Porgy

Porgy

A GULLAH VERSION

by
Virginia Mixson Geraty

From the original play
by
Dorothy Heyward
and
DuBose Heyward

Wyrick & Company
CHARLESTON

The author and publisher wish to thank the DuBose and Dorothy Heyward Memorial Fund for a grant to the College of Charleston which assisted in the publication of this book.

Published by Wyrick & Company
        Post Office Box 89
        Charleston, South Carolina 29402

The original version of *Porgy,* a Play In Four Acts, was published in 1927 for The Theatre Guild by Doubleday, Page & Company, New York.

Library of Congress Cataloging-In-Publication Data

Heyward, Dorothy, 1890-1961
        [Porgy. Gullah & English]
        Porgy: a play in four acts/by Dorothy Heyward and DuBose
        Heyward, from the novel by DuBose Heyward; Gullah transla-
        tion by Virginia Mixson Geraty.
                p. cm.
        Descriptions and stage directions in English; dialogue in
        Gullah.
        ISBN 0-941711-11-0: $8.95
        I. Heyward, DuBose, 1885-1940. II. Title.
        PS3515.E97P613 1989
        812'.52—dc20
                                        89-38028
                                        CIP

ISBN 0-941711-11-0

FOREWORD

This Gullah version of *Porgy* has been a long time in the works. The idea presented itself many years ago when I found that the dialogue of the play had not been written in the delightful, old Gullah Language.

For several weeks I had waited, impatiently, for my copy of *Porgy*. When it finally arrived, I quickly scanned the introductory pages, and went directly to Act One. The setting had been skillfully done in fine detail. I felt as though I were actually there among the residents of Catfish Row, waiting for the craps game to begin. Then, the let down! Jake spoke the opening lines.

I can't begin to describe my disappointment when I found that the dialogue was not written in the language which would have been used by the black people living in Catfish Row. Confused and disconcerted by the words and expressions which were used to portray the thoughts of the characters, I closed the book and put it away. However, by the next evening I was well into the translation of *Porgy*.

Since Gullah is a creole language which was never intended to be written, there are no concrete rules governing its grammar. But since it is English-based, its vocabulary is mostly English, with only a few African words reminiscent of its early pidgin status.

There are, however, many syntactical features in common with West African English-derived creoles, and a certain flavor of the West African Coast in its intonation and stress. Gullah is spoken softly, with a rolling rhythm. As Gullah people speak, you can almost hear the wind ruffling the marsh grasses. The words sway like the moss that hangs from the live oak trees.

Having lived among the Gullah people for the greater part of my life, I find no difficulty in understanding their language and in reproducing on paper the sounds that fall so easily from the Gullah tongue. Besides an interesting and extensive vocabulary, this language is rich in idiomatic expressions. The frequent use of idioms is one of the most attractive features of Gullah, and at the same time, the feature which makes the language so difficult to comprehend.

In the preparation of this Gullah version of *Porgy*, I have in no way altered the theme of the play. The changes I have made have to do with the dialogue, and apply to idiom, orthography, and sentence structure. To facilitate the reader's understanding and appreciation of this book, I have provided a glossary and an explanation of some word usages.

Needless to say, I have truly enjoyed doing this translation. Many years have passed since I first became motivated to rewrite the dialogue of *Porgy*. And, now, in the autumn of my life, I am finally able to realize my ambition.

My primary purpose in this work, and in all my work with Gullah, is to increase public awareness of the language and to generate more interest in the preservation of this unique contribution to our American heritage from the Afro-American people.

I am grateful to Mr. Louis H. Aborn of Tams-Witmark Music Library, Inc. for having obtained permission from the Trustee for the Heyward family for me to do this work. Also, I wish to thank Mr. William McG. Morrison, Jr., Professor Eugene C. Hunt, Mr. Charles W. Joyner, and Colonel D.T. Ouzts for their interest and support. Sincere thanks go to Mr. Thomas Raines, Deputy Director of the Charleston County Library for allowing me to borrow from the Charleston Room the very dear and special copy of *Porgy* which had belonged to Janie Screven Heyward.

I sincerely hope that the Heyward heirs are pleased with this Gullah version of *Porgy!*

Virginia Mixson Geraty

Charleston, South Carolina

CHARACTERS

MARIA, keeper of the cookshop
JAKE, captain of the fishing fleet
LILY
MINGO
ANNIE
SPORTING LIFE
SERENA, Robbin's wife
ROBBINS, a young stevedore
JIM
CLARA, Jake's wife
PETER, the honey-man
PORGY, a crippled beggar
CROWN, a stevedore
CROWN'S BESS
A DETECTIVE
TWO POLICEMEN
UNDERTAKER
SCIPIO
SIMON FRAZIER, a lawyer
NELSON, a fisherman
ALAN ARCHDALE
THE CRAB MAN
THE CORONER
RESIDENTS OF CATFISH ROW,
FISHERMEN, CHILDREN, STEVEDORES, ETC.

*The action of the play takes place
in Charleston S.C.*

SYNOPSIS OF SCENES

ACT I
Scene I — Catfish Row. A Summer Evening.
Scene II — Serena's Room. The Following Night.
(Intermission five minutes)

ACT II
Scene I — Catfish Row. A Month Later.
Scene II — A Palmetto Jungle. Evening the Same Day.
(Intermission ten minutes)

ACT III
Scene I — Catfish Row. Before Dawn. A Week Later.
Scene II — Serena's Room. Dawn of the Following Day.

ACT IV
Scene I — Catfish Row. The Next Night.
Scene II — Catfish Row. The Next Afternoon
Scene III — Catfish Row. Five Days Later

PORGY

ACT ONE

PORGY

ACT ONE

Scene One

Before the rise of each curtain, the bells of St. Michael's,
adjacent to the Negro quarter of old Charleston, chime the hour.
The chimes are heard occasionally throughout the play.

Before the rise of first curtain, St. Michael's chimes the
quarters and strikes eight.

The curtain rises on the court of Catfish Row, now a Negro
tenement in a fallen quarter of Charleston, but in Colonial days
one of the finest buildings of the aristocracy. The walls rise
around a court, except a part of the rear wall of the old house,
which breaks to leave a section of lower wall pierced at its centre
by a massive wrought-iron gate of great beauty which hangs
unsteadily between brick pillars surmounted by pineapples carved
of Italian marble.

By day, the walls of the entire structure present a mottled
colour effect of varying pastel shades, caused by the atmospheric
action on many layers of colour wash. A brilliant note is added by
rows of blooming flame-coloured geraniums in old vegetable tins
on narrow shelves attached to each window sill. All of the windows are equipped with dilapidated slat shutters, some of which
are open, others closed, but with the slats turned so that anyone
inside could look out without being seen. The floor of the spacious
court is paved with large flagstones, and these gleam in faintly
varying colours under their accumulated grime.

Beyond the gate and above the wall, one sees a littered cob-
bled street, an old gas street lamp, and, beyond that again, the
blue expanse of the bay with Fort Sumter showing on the horizon.

Over the wall can be seen masts and spars of fishing boats lying on the beach.

By night, the court depends for its illumination upon the wheezing gas lamp, and the kerosene lamps and lanterns that come and go in the hands of the occupants of the Row.

At left front is PORGY'S *room (door and window), and beyond it, an arch letting on an inside yard. The pump stands against the wall right back; then, on around right wall,* SERENA'S *doorway, with her window above it, two more doors, then the door to* MARIA'S *cookshop. Centre right is seen* SERENA'S *wash bench, and near the right wall, well down front, is table on which* MARIA *serves her meals during the warm weather.*

As the curtain rises, revealing Catfish Row on a summer evening, the court reechoes with African laughter and friendly banter in "Gullah," the language of the Charleston Negro, which still retains many African words. The audience understands none of it. Like the laughter and movement, the twanging of a guitar from an upper window,the dancing of an urchin with a loose, shuffling step, it is a part of the picture of Catfish Row as it really is — an alien scene, a people as little known to most Americans as the people of the Congo.

It is Saturday night, and most of the residents of Catfish Row are out in the court, sitting watching the crap shooters or moving to and fro to visit with one neighbour, then another. Among those present are:

MARIA, *matriarch of the court, massive in proportions and decisive in action.*

ANNIE, *middle-aged, quiet, and sedate.*

LILY, *loud, good-natured, the court hoyden.*

CLARA, *who has her baby in her arms. She is scarcely more than a girl and has a sweet, wistful face.*

JAKE, CLARA'S *husband. A successful captain of the fishing fleet; good-looking, good-natured.*
"SPORTING LIFE," *bootlegger to Catfish Row, a slender, over-dressed, high-yellow Negro.*
MINGO, *young and lazy.*
JIM *and* NELSON, *fishermen.*
SCIPIO, *a boy of twelve, one of the numerous offspring of* ROBBINS *and* SERENA.

ROBBINS *and* SERENA *are still in their room on second floor.* SERENA *is seen occasionally as she moves back and forth past her lighted window. She is a self-respecting "white folks" negress, of about thirty.*
The men are gathering for their Saturday-night crap game. They are grouped between gate and PORGY'S *room.* JAKE *is squatting right,* MINGO *center rear, and* SPORTING LIFE *is left, forming triangle. A smoking kerosene lamp is in centre of group, and the men are tossing and retrieving their dice in the circle of light.*

JAKE: [*Rolling*]:'E seem lukkuh dese bone ent gimme nutt'n' 'cep' boxcyaa' tenight. 'E stan'so de two week gone, w'en de game bruk me. Uh ent luk dat kinduh luck!

[SPORTING LIFE *produces his own dice, and throws with a loud grunt and snap of his fingers.* MINGO *snatches the dice and balances them in his hand.*]

SPORTING LIFE: Dam' you, gimme dem bone! [MINGO *holds him off with one hand while he hands the dice to* JAKE.]

MINGO: Jake, wuh you say 'bout dese?

JAKE: [*Examining them*]: Dem de same cockeye bone wuh clean out de gang las' week. Ef dey roll een dis game, Uh gwi' roll out. [*Hands the dice back to* SPORTING

LIFE.]: Eb'rybody roll de same bone een dis game. Tek 'um eeduhso lef' um, Spo't'n' Life.

[ROBBINS *comes from door, near right. He is a well-set-up Negro of about thirty. The window above him opens, and* SERENA *leans from sill.*]

SERENA: [*Pleadingly*]: Honey Boy!

ROBBINS: Fuh Gawd sake, don' staa't dat 'gen. Uh gwi' play, you yeddy?

SERENA: Ef you ent hab likkuh een you, you ent fuh talk dat way. You 'membuh wuh you prommus me las' week, enty?

ROBBINS: Berrywellden, Uh yent gwi' shoot but fufty cent. [*Joins the group.*]

[CLARA *paces up and down the court, singing softly to her baby.*] Me ole 'ooman min' run on jine de bury'n' laa'ge. Uh suh spen'um w'ile you 'libe en' kick'n'.

[*Picks up dice. Throws them with a loud grunt.*] Uh yent see no buzzut duh grin'salt 'roun' yuh.

[JIM, *a big, strong-looking fellow, saunters over to the group of crap players. A cotton hook swings from his belt.*]

JIM: Lawd, Uh too w'ary dis night. Uh duh t'ink 'bout lef' de cott'n bidness. 'E awright fuh uh nigguh luk Crown wuh Gawd staa't fuh mek'um bull, den 'E change 'E min'. But 'e yent no wu'k fuh man.

JAKE: Come 'long wid me en' de Sea Gull. Uh need anudduh fish man.

JIM: Fuh true? Sho'nuf dis cott'n hook done swing 'e las' bale. You wan' dis cott'n hook, Scipio?

[*Throws the hook to* SCIPIO, *who takes it eagerly, fastens it at his waist, and goes about court playing that he is a stevedore, lifting objects with the hook and pretending that they are of tremendous weight.* CLARA *passes the group, crooning softly.*]

CLARA: "Hush leetle baby, don' you cry. You farruh en' murruh bin bawn tuh die."

JAKE: [*Standing up*]: Dat chile ent duh sleep yet? G'em yuh, Uh kin fix'um. [*Takes baby from* CLARA, *rocks it in his arms and sings*]:
"Me mammy done tell me, long time ago,
Son don' you marri'd no gal you know.
Spen' all you money, eat all you bread,
Gone tuh Sabannuh, lef' you fuh dead."

[*Several of the men join in on the last line.* JAKE *rocks the baby more violently and begins to shuffle.* CLARA *watches anxiously.*]
"Spen' all you money. T'ief all you clo'es.
Wuh gwi' come ub you, Gawd only knows.

[*The light leaves* SERENA'S *window.* JAKE *swings the baby back to* CLARA.]
Wuh Uh tell you! 'E done duh sleep!

[*The baby wails. The men laugh.* CLARA *carries baby to her room. Closes door.* SERENA *comes from her door with a lamp which she sets on her wash bench. She sits beside it and looks anxiously toward crap players.*]

MARIA: [*To* SERENA]: Mek you duh worry so? You hab one de bes' mens een Catfish Row. Mek you ent leh'um play bidout you 'taguhnize'um?

SERENA: Robbin hab likkuh een'um tenight. 'E yent de same man w'en 'e hab likkuh een'um.

[MINGO *is rolling and retrieving the dice. While he does so, he looks and laughs at* ROBBINS, *then sings at him.*]

MINGO: [*Singing*]:
"Me mammy done tell me, long time ago,
Son don' you marri'd no gal you know."
[*Speaking to* ROBBINS]: Oughtuh single luk Porgy en' me. Den
    you kin shoot bone bidout 'ooman 'buze you.

ROBBINS: Me 'ooman awright, 'cep' 'e yent luk crap. 'E bin
    bawn uh w'ite-folk nigguh. 'E people, dem, blan blonx tuh
    Gubnuh Raatlaige. Ent you see Mis' Raatlaige come'fuh
    shum w'en 'e sick?

MARIA: [*Overhearing, to* SERENA]: Dat bin Mis' Raatlaige wuh
    come'fuh'see you?

SERENA: 'E stan'so! You ent know dat?

MARIA: 'E ebbuh sell enny 'e ole clo'es?

SERENA: 'E ent sell'um, 'cep' sometime 'e g'em tuh nigguh.

MARIA: [*Sighing*]: Uh sho' wish uh bin hab one 'e dress. 'E de
    fus' pussun uh see hab hip en' bus' stan' same lukkuh
    me'own.

ROBBINS: [*Boasting*]: Yaas, suh! Me lady!

SPORTING LIFE: You bes' sabe you sweetmout' talk fuh dem
    dice. Bone ent hab no pashunt wid 'ooman.

MINGO: Dat de trute. 'Co'se dey cyan' git 'long tuhgedduh.
    Dem alltwo attuh de same nigguh money, enty?

JAKE: Annie, you luk de single life, enty? Weh dat ole fish man
    wuh nyuse tuh come'fuh see you?

ANNIE: 'E ent no fish man!
JAKE: Wuh 'e do?

ANNIE: 'E yent do nutt'n', de mo'res'. Sometime 'e duh men'
    shoe.

[*The voice of* PETER, *the old "honey man," is heard in the street, drawing nearer and nearer.*]

PETER: Yuh come de honey man. You hab honey? — Yaas, ma'am, Uh hab honey. — You hab honey een de comb? — Yaas, ma'am, Uh hab honey een de comb. You hab honey cheap? — Yaas, ma'am me honey cheap.

[PETER *enters gate and closes it behind him. He is a gentle, kindly Negro, verging on senility. A large wooden tray covered with a white cloth is balanced on his head.*]

LILY: [*Going to meet him*]: Well yuh come me ole man. [*Takes tray from his head and shouts in his ear*]: Weh de money?

[*He hands her some coins. She points to bench.*] Now, go set tuh oneside en' res'. [*He does as he is told. She places tray in her room and returns to circle.*]

MARIA: Come'yuh, Scipio! Yuh come Porgy op'n de gate!

[PORGY *drives up to the gate in his soap-box chariot. He is a crippled beggar of the Charleston streets, who has done much to overcome his handicap of almost powerless legs by supplying himself with a patriarchal and very dirty goat, which draws a cart made of an upturned soap box, on two lopsided wheels, which bears the inscription,* "WILD ROSE SOAP, PURE AND FRAGRANT."]

PORGY *is no longer young, and yet not old. There is a suggestion of the mystic in his thoughtful, sensitive face. He is black, with the almost purple blackness of unadulterated Congo blood.*

SCIPIO *reluctantly interrupts his performance on a mouth organ, shuffles across court, and opens one side of the ponderous gate.*

PORGY *drives through and pulls up beside the crap ring.*]

JAKE: Yuh come de ole crap man!

PORGY: Awright Mingo! Jake! he'p me out dis waggin. Uh hab 'nuf de buckruh money, en' ennybody kin hab'um wuh able fuh tek'um f'um Porgy.

[MINGO *and* JAKE *help* PORGY *from wagon to a seat on ground at left front of circle.* SCIPIO *leads goat away through arch at rear left.*]

[JIM *saunters to gate and looks out.*]

ROBBINS: Awright, mens! Roll'um! Us done was'e 'nuf time.

JIM: [*Returning to group*]: Us bes' wait fuh Crown. Uh shum duh come 'long duh tek de whole sidewalk, en' 'e look luk 'e yent gwi' stan' fuh no fool.

PORGY: 'E hab Bess wid'um?

JAKE: Liss'n tuh Porgy! 'E mus'e lub Crown Bess!

[*All men laugh.*]

PORGY: Gawd mek cripple fuh lonesome. Ent no nyuse fuhr'um lub 'ooman.

MARIA: Porgy smaa't tummuch fuh look 'pun dat likkuh-guzzl'n' slut.

LILY: Likkuh? 'E tek mo'nuh likkuh fuh sattify Bess.

SERENA: Happy dus'! Dat wuh 'e tek! Dat gal Bess ent fit fuh sosh'ate wid Gawd-fayr'n' lady.

SPORTING LIFE: Sistuh, you ent haffuh worry! Gawd- fayr'n' lady de las' t'ing on eart' Bess wan' sosh'ate wid.

PORGY: Mek you ent stop onrabble you mout' 'bout Bess? Twix de Gawd-fayr'n' lady and en' de Gawd-dam'n' mens, dat gal ent hab no chance!

JAKE: Ent uh tell you Porgy lub'um?

[More laughter.]

PORGY: Uh ent nebbuh crack me teet' tuhr'um.

[CROWN *and* BESS *appear at gate.* CROWN *is lurching slightly and* BESS *is piloting him through the entrance.*

CROWN *is a huge Negro of magnificent physique, a stevedore on the cotton wharfs. He is wearing blue denim pants and tan shirt with a bright bandanna about his neck. From his belt hangs a long gleaming cotton hook.*

BESS *is slender, but sinewy; very black, wide nostrils, and large, but well-formed mouth. She flaunts a typical, but debased, Negro beauty.*

From the occupants of Catfish Row there are cries of, "Yuh come Big Boy!" "'Lo, Crown!" "'Lo, Bess!"

CROWN: [*To* SPORTING LIFE]: Awright, soon-man. Gib'we uh pint, en' mek'um dam' quick!

[SPORTING LIFE *pulls a flask from his hip pocket and hands it to* CROWN. CROWN *jerks out cork and takes a long pull.*] [*To* BESS]: Pay'um, Bess!

[BESS *settles for the bottle, then takes her seat by* CROWN, *ignoring the women of the court.*

CROWN *hands her the flask, from which she takes a long pull. She meets* SERENA'S *eyes, laughs at their hostility, and at once extends the bottle to* ROBBINS.]

BESS: Hab one fuh de Gawd-fayr'n' lady. Dey ent nutt'n' else lukkuh dem, t'engk Gawd!

[ROBBINS *tries to resist, but the fumes of raw liquor are too much for him. He takes a deep drink.*

CROWN *snatches the bottle from him, gulps the entire remaining contents, and shatters it on the flags behind him.*

The crap circle is now complete. The positions are as follows:

Rear

X BESS X CROWN X DADDY PETER X MINGO X SPORTING LIFE
X JAKE X ROBBINS X PORGY

Footlights

[CROWN *throws coin down before him.*]

CROWN: Uh duh talk tuh oonuh mens. Ennybody gwi' mek ansuh?

[*They all throw down money.*]

ROBBINS: [*To* JAKE]: En' me fine chillun, dem!

CROWN: Tie up you dam' mout', en' t'row!

ROBBINS: [*Taken aback and rolling hastily*]: Boxcyaa' 'gen!

[*They all roar with laughter.*]

MINGO: Kibbuhr'um, bubbuh, kibbuhr'um!

ROBBINS: Kibbuhr'um hell! Uh gwi' pass'um 'long en' see kin uh bruk me luck.

MINGO: 'E lady ent 'low'um but fufty cent, en' 'e cyan' tek no chance.

[*All laugh at* ROBBINS.]

BESS: [*With a provocative look at* SERENA]: Nemmin', Honey-boy, Uh kin stake you w'en you fo' bit done gone.

SERENA: [*To* ROBBINS]: Go 'head en' play, you ent need no he'p f'um no she-debble.

BESS: [*To* ROBBINS]: See wuh Uh do fuh you? De she- gawd easy fuh 'suade w'en you know huffuh 'suade'um. [CROWN *claps his hand over* BESS'S *mouth.*]

CROWN: Tie you dam' mout'! Don' gib' Mingo chance fuh talk tuh de bone.

[JAKE *has cast and lost, and the dice are now with* MINGO, *who is swinging them back and forth in his hand. Sings.*]

MINGO: "Ole snake-eye, gone off en' die.
Ole man seb'n, come down f'um Heb'n."
[*Grunts, throws, and snaps fingers.*] [*Scoops up dice.*]

CROWN: Uh yent see no seb'n. [*Snatches* MINGO'S *hand and opens fingers. Looks at dice.*] You done tu'n'um obuh!

MINGO: [*To Circle*]: Wuh dat Uh t'row? [*Cries of* "Seb'n," "Jis' luk 'e suh," *etc.* MINGO *pulls in pot.*]

CROWN: Uh suh mo'nuh one nigguh done meet 'e Gawd fuh pull'um een 'fo' uh read'um! En' Uh sesso 'gen tenight.

[*All ante again.*]

MINGO: Come'yuh tuh you pappy. [*Shoots.*] Fo'tuh mek! Come fo'! [*Shoots.*] [*Cries of* "Seb'n," "Crap out," *etc.* MINGO *passes dice to* CROWN.]

CROWN: Come clean, alltwo you black-eye bitch! [*Shoots.*] [*Cries of* "Six," "Six tuh mek." CROWN *takes up bones and produces rabbit foot from pocket. He touches dice with it.*] Kiss rabbit foot! [*Shoots.*]

SPORTING LIFE: [*Reaching for dice*]: Crap out! Come tuh you pappy.

[CROWN *extends a huge arm and brushes him back. He tries to focus his eyes on dice.*]

ROBBINS: Crown too cockeye drunk fuh read'um. Wuh 'e suh Bess?

BESS: Seb'n.

CROWN [*Scowls at* ROBBINS, *then turns to* SPORTING LIFE.]: Uh yent drunk 'nuf fuh read'um. Dat de trubble. Likkuh ent dat strong. Gimme uh tetch ub happy dus', Spo't'n' Life.

[SPORTING LIFE *takes from his pocket a small folded paper.*]

BESS: Spo't'n' Life, don' g'em dat stuff. 'E done awready oagly drunk.

CROWN: You duh talk! Pay'um en' shet up! [*Takes the paper from* SPORTING LIFE, *unfolds it, and inhales the powder.*

BESS *pays* SPORTING LIFE. DADDY PETER *takes his pipe from his mouth and crowds in between* CROWN *and* SPORTING LIFE, *putting a hand on the arm of each.*]

PETER: Fr'en' en' dice en' happy dus' ent mek fuh sosh'ate. Oonuh bes' go slow!

[CROWN *draws back his fist. Cries of* "Lef' Uncle Petuh 'lone!" "'E yent mean no haa'm!" CROWN *relaxes.* SPORTING LIFE *picks up the dice.*]

SPORTING LIFE: Yuh seb'n! Yuh seb'n! Yuh seb'n! [*Shoots.*] 'Leb'n! Come home, Fido! [*Whistles, snaps fingers, and pulls in pot.*]

[*All ante.*]

CROWN: Gaw'dam'it! Uh yent read'um yet!

[*All laugh at him. Cries of* "Crown cockeye drunk." "Cyan' tell dice f'um watuhmilyun," *etc.*]

CROWN: [*Growling*]: Awright, Uh done tell you!

SPORTING LIFE: [*Shooting*]: Six tuh mek! Git'um'gen. [*Shoots.*] [*Cries of* "Seb'n," "Crap out," *etc.* PORGY *takes up dice and commences to sway, with his eyes half closed. He apostrophizes dice in a sort of sing-song chant.*]

PORGY: Oh, leetle staar, roll me some light. [*Shoots.*] 'Leb'n lettle staar, come home. [*Pulls in pot.*] [*All ante.*] Roll dis po' baiguh uh sun en' uh moon! [*Shoots.*]

MINGO: Snake eye!

PORGY: Dat ent no snake eye. Dat uh crop ub mawn'n en' eben'n staar. Watch'um rise fuh dis po' baiguh! [*Shoots.*] [*Cries of* "'E mek'um," "Dat 'e p'int," *etc.* PORGY *pulls in pot.*]

CROWN: Roll up you sleebe, nigguh!
[PORGY *rolls up his sleeves.*]
Wellden, you hab de dam' dice cunjuh!

[*All ante.* PORGY *rolls. Cries of* "Snake eye," "Crap out!" *All ante.* ROBBINS *takes up bones, whistles, shoots, snaps them back up very rapidly.*]

ROBBINS: Nine tuh mek! [*Whistles, shoots, snaps fingers.*] Read de nine! [*Sweeps them up, and reaches for money.* CROWN *seizes his wrist.*]

CROWN: Tetch dat money en' you meet you Gawd!

ROBBINS: Tek you han' off me, you low houn'!
[*To* JAKE.] Han' me dat brick behime you!

[JAKE *reaches brickbat and puts it in his free hand.* CROWN *jerks his cotton hook out of his belt and lunges forward, bowling* ROBBINS *over, and knocking brick from his hand.* CROWN *then steps back and kicks over lamp, extinguishing it.*

The stage is now dark except for the small lamp at SERENA'S *wash bench. This lights up the woman's terrified face as she strains her gaze into the darkness.*

MARIA, CLARA *and the other of her group stand behind her.*

From the crap ring come cries and curses.

Suddenly, shutters are thrown open in right and left walls of building, and forms strain from the sills. As the shutters are banged open, shafts of light from them flash across the court, latticing it with a cross-play of light.

CROWN *and* ROBBINS *are revealed facing each other:* CROWN *crouched for a spring with gleaming cotton hook extended;* ROBBINS *defenseless, his back to the wall.*

Then ROBBINS *lunges under the hook and they clinch. The fight proceeds with no distinguishable words from the combatants, but with bestial growls and breath that sobs and catches in their throats. In and out of the cross-play of light they sway — now revealed, now in darkness. The watchers move back and stand around the wall. They commence a weird, high- keyed moaning that rises as the figures take the light, and subsides almost to silence when they are obscured.*

Suddenly, out of the dark, CROWN *swings* ROBBINS *into a shaft of light.* CROWN *is facing the audience and is holding* ROBBINS *by the throat at arms' length. With a triumphant snarl, he swings the hook downward.*

ROBBINS *drops back toward audience into darkness, and* CROWN *stands in high light.*

There is dead silence now. In it CROWN *looks down at his hands, opening and closing them. Then he draws his arm across his eyes.*

The silence is shattered by a piercing scream, and SERENA *runs across the court and throws herself on the body.*

BESS *appears in the light beside* CROWN. *She shakes him violently by the arm.*]

BESS: Mek'ace en' light out. You ent hab time fuh loss!

CROWN: [*Looking stupidly into the gloom at* SERENA *and the body of her man*]: Wuh you duh talk 'bout?

BESS: [*Hysterically*]: You done kill Robbin, en' de poleece gwi' come, fuh sho'! [*She starts to pull him toward the gate.*]

CROWN: Weh you gwi' hide? Eb'rybody know us pull tuhged-duh.

[*In the half light, it can now be seen that the court has been deserted, except for* SERENA, *who sits beside the body with her head bowed, and sways from side to side with a low, steady moaning.*

A match is scratched and held in PORGY'S *hand. He is crouched on his doorstep. He looks toward* ROBBINS'S *body, and his face shows horror and fear. He gives a whimpering moan, and as the match burns out, he drags himself over his threshold and closes the door.*]

BESS: Dey ent gwi' look fuh me yuh. Uh gwi' hide right yuh. Somebody gwi' tek cyah ub Bess.

CROWN: [*Now at gate*]: Dat somebody ent fuh good! Uh gwi' come back w'en de trubble obuh.

BESS: Berrywell, tek dis en' mek'ace!
[*Thrusts the money into his hand. She pushes him out of gate. He disappears into the shadows. She turns around and faces the court. It is silent and empty except for the body and* SERENA. SPORTING LIFE *steps out of the shadows under* SERENA'S *steps, startling her.*]
Dat you, Spo't'n' Life? Fuh Gawd sake gimme uh leetle tetch uh happy dus'. Uh duh shake so uh haa'dly'kin stan'. [*Suddenly remembering*]: Uh cyan' pay fuhr'um. Uh done gib' all de money tuh Crown. But, fuh Gawd sake gimme uh tetch!

SPORTING LIFE: You ent haffuh pay fuhr'um. [*Pours powder into her hand.*] Uh yent gwi' 'bandun you lukkuh dese odduh no'count nigguh.

[BESS *quickly inhales the powder. Sighs with relief.*] Liss'n! Uh gwine tuh New Yawk soon. Ef you come wid me now, Uh kin hide you en' cya' you 'long w'en Uh go. Us gwi' mek uh fine team. Wid you looks, en' me fr'en' dey dey, us hab likkuh, dus', paa'ty en't'ing eb'ry night 'tell dayclean. [*He looks apprehensively toward gate. Takes her arm.*] Come leh we go, w'ile de goin' good! [BESS *draws away sharply from his grasp.*] Ent nobody 'roun' yuh gwi' tek een Crown 'ooman! You bes' come 'long wid you one fr'en'.

BESS: Uh yent come tuh dat yet!

SPORTING LIFE: Berrywell, de poleece ent gwi' fin' me yuh! [*Slinks out gate.*]

[BESS *looks desperately about for shelter. She advances timidly and takes up lamp from the wash bench. She starts at rear left, and tries all of the doors as she goes. They are either locked, or slammed in her face as she reaches out to them. She comes to* MARIA'S *shop door, and as she reaches it, it is jerked open and* MARIA *confronts her.*]

MARIA: [*In a tense voice*]: You done cause 'nuffuh trubble. Go'way 'fo' de patrol git yuh!

BESS: You cyan' hab mussy on me, en' tek me een?

MARIA: Hell kin freeze fus'!

[*A light is lit in* PORGY'S *room, showing at window and crack in door.*]

BESS: [*Indicating* PORGY'S *room*]: Who dat lib' obuh yanduh?

MARIA: Ent no use fuh you gone obuh yanduh. Porgy lib' dey. 'E uh cripple baiguh.

[BESS *seems to agree with* MARIA *that* PORGY *is of no use to her. Crosses to gate, hesitates. Then she turns slowly toward* POR-GY'S *room and crosses, shuddering away from* SERENA *and the body, which she must pass on the way. She reaches the door, puts her hand on the knob, hesitates, then slowly she opens it, enters, and closes it behind her.*]

CURTAIN

Scene Two

St. Michael's chimes the quarters and strikes seven.

The curtain rises on SERENA'S *room, a second story room in Catfish Row, which still bears traces of its ancient beauty in its high panelled walls and tall, slender mantel with Grecian frieze and intricate scroll work. The door is in left wall at back. Near the centre of back wall a window looks toward the sea. The fireplace is in right wall. Over the mantel is a gaudy lithograph of Lincoln striking chains from the slaves.*

The room is vaguely lighted by several kerosene lamps, and is scantily furnished: a bed against the back wall at left, and a few chairs.

ROBBINS'S *body lies upon the bed, completely covered by a white sheet. On its chest is a large blue saucer. Standing about the bed or seated on the floor are Negroes, all singing and swaying and patting with their large feet.*

SERENA *sits at the foot of the bed swaying dismally to the rhythm.*

They have been singing for hours. The monotony of the dirge and the steady beat of the patting has lulled several into a state of coma.
"De't' ent you hab no shame, shame?
De't' ent you hab no shame, shame?
De't' ent you hab no shame, shame?
De't' ent you hab no shame?

Tek dis man en' gone, gone,
Tek dis man en' gone, gone,
Tek dis man en' gone, gone,
De't' ent you hab no shame?

Lef' dis 'ooman 'lone, 'lone,
Lef' dis 'ooman 'lone, 'lone,
Lef' dis 'ooman 'lone, 'lone,
De't' ent you hab no shame?"

[*The door opens and* PETER *comes in. Doffs his old hat, crosses, and puts coins in saucer. The singing and swaying continue. He finds a seat at right front and begins to sway and pat with the others.*

SERENA *reaches over, gets saucer, and counts coins. Replaces saucer with a hopeless expression.*]

JAKE: How de saucuh stan', Sistuh? [*The singing dies gradually as, one by one, the Negroes stop to listen, but the rhythm continues.*]

SERENA: [*Dully*]: Fo'teen dolluh en' t'irty-six cent.

MARIA: [*Encouragingly*]: 'E com'n' 'long, Sistuh. You kin bury'um soon.

SERENA: De Boa'd ub He'lt' suh Uh haffuh bury'um tuhmor-ruh.

CLARA: 'E cos' t'irty-fo' dollah fuh bury me gramma, but us hab t'ree cyaaridge.

SERENA: Wuh Uh gwi' do ef Uh ent hab de money?

PETER: [*Understanding that they refer to saucer*]: Gawd hab' 'nuf money fuh de saucuh.

SERENA: Bress de Lawd!

PETER: En' 'E gwi' saa'f' dese nigguh haa't fuh full de saucuh 'tell 'e run obuh.

SERENA: Amen, me Jedus!

PETER: De Lawd gwi' puhwide grabe fuh 'E chillun.

CLARA: Bress de Lawd! [*The swaying gradually changes to the rhythm of* PETER'S *prayer.*]

PETER: 'E gwi' cumfut de widduh!

SERENA: Oh, me Jedus!

PETER: En' puhwide bittle fuh de chillun.

SERENA: Yaas, Lawd!

PETER: 'E gwi' raise dis po' nigguh out 'e grabe.

JAKE: Hallylooyuh!

PETER: En' set'um een de riteshus seat.

SERENA: Amen, me bredduh. [*They all sway in silence.*]

ANNIE: [*Looking toward door*]: Wuh dat iz?

CLARA: Uh yeddy somebody come up de step duh bring penny fuh de saucuh.

[MARIA *opens the door and looks out.*]

SERENA: Who 'e yiz?

MARIA: Porgy duh come up de step!

JAKE: [*Starting to rise*]: Somebody bes' go fuh he'p'um.

MARIA: 'E hab he'p. Bess duh he'p'um.

SERENA: [*Springing to her feet*]: Wuffuh Bess duh come'yuh? [*They are all silent, looking toward door.* PORGY *and* BESS *enter.* PORGY *looks about; makes a movement toward corpse.* BESS *starts to lead him across room.* SERENA *stands defiant, silent, till they have gone half the way.*] W'ymekso you fetch dat 'ooman yuh?

PORGY: 'E wan' he'p sing. 'E know good huffuh shout. [BESS, *self-possessed, leads* PORGY *on toward saucer. He deposits his coins. Then* BESS *stretches her hand toward saucer.*]

SERENA: Uh yent need you money fuh bury me man! [BESS *hesitates*.] Uh yent wan' no money f'um de man wuh kill'um.

PORGY: Dat ent Crown money. Uh gib' Bess money fuh pit een de saucuh.

SERENA: Berrywellden, you kin pit'um een.

[BESS *drops the money in saucer and leads* PORGY *to a place at left front. They sit side by side on the floor.* SERENA *stands glaring after them.*]

PETER: [*Trying to make peace*]: Hice un chune, Sistuh! Time duh was'e en' de saucuh stillyet ent fill.

SERENA: [*To* PORGY]: Bess kin seddown obuh een de cawnuh ef 'e wantuh. 'Cep'n' 'e cyan' sing!

[BESS *sits with quiet dignity; seeming scarcely to notice* SERENA'S *tone and words.*]

PORGY: Nemmin', Bess ent wan' sing nohow!
[*The spiritual begins again.*]
"Lef' dese chillun fuh staa'b, staa'b,
Lef' dese chillun fuh staa'b, staa'b,
Lef' dese chillun fuh staa'b, staa'b,
De't' ent you hab no shame?"

MINGO: [*Looking upward*]: Dat rain Uh yeddy?

JAKE: Yaas, 'e duh rain haa'd, fuh true!

PORGY: Dat good fuh Robbin. Gawd done sen' rain fuh wash 'e foot-step f'um de eart'.

LILY: Oh yaas, Brudduh!

SERENA: Amen, me Jedus!

[*The spiritual continues. The swaying and patting begin gradu-*

ally and grow. Slowly BESS *begins to sway with the others,
but she makes no sound.*

The door is burst suddenly open and the DETECTIVE *enters.* TWO
POLICEMEN *wait in the doorway.*

*The spiritual ceases abruptly. All the Negroes' eyes are riveted on
the white man and filled with fear. He strides over to the
corpse, looks down at it.*]

DETECTIVE: Um! A saucer-buried nigguh, I see! [*To*
SERENA]: You're his widow?

SERENA: Yaas, suh.

DETECTIVE: He didn't leave any burial insurance?

SERENA: No, suh, Boss. 'E ent lef' nutt'n'.

DETECTIVE: Well, see to it that he's buried tomorrow. [*Turns
away from her. Slowly circles room, looking fixedly at each
Negro in turn. Each quails under his gaze. He pauses
abruptly before* PETER. *Suddenly shouts at him*]: You killed
Robbins, and I'm going to hang you for it!

[PETER *is almost paralyzed by terror, his panic heightened by the
fact that he cannot hear what the* DETECTIVE *says. His
mouth opens and he cannot find his voice.*]

LILY: [*To* DETECTIVE]: Petuh ent do'um!

PETER: [*Helplessly*]: Wuh 'e suh?

LILY: [*Shouting in* PETER'S *ear*]: 'E suh you done kill Robbin.

DETECTIVE: [*Laying his hand on* PETER'S *shoulder*]: Come
along now!

PETER: Swaytogawd, Boss, Uh yent do'um!

[*The* DETECTIVE *whips out his revolver and points it between*
PETER'S *eyes.*]

DETECTIVE: Who did it then? [*Shouting.*] You heard me! Who did it?

PETER: [*Wildly*]: Crown do'um! Uh shum! Crown do'um!

DETECTIVE: [*Shouting*]: You're sure you saw him?

PETER: Swaytogawd, boss. Uh bin right dey nex' tuhr'um.

DETECTIVE: [*With satisfied grunt*]: Umph! I thought as much. [*Swings suddenly on* PORGY *and points the pistol in his face.*] You saw it, too! [PORGY *trembles but does not speak. He lowers his eyes.*] Come! Out with it! I don't want to have to put the law on you! [PORGY *sits silent. The* DETECTIVE *shouts with fury.*] Look at me, you damned nigger! [PORGY *slowly raises his eyes to the* DETECTIVE'S *face.*]

PORGY: Uh yent know nutt'n' 'bout'um, Boss!

DETECTIVE: [*Angrily*]: That's your room in the corner, isn't it? [*Points downward toward left.*]

PORGY: Yaas'suh, Boss, dat me room!

DETECTIVE: The door opens on the court, don't it?

PORGY: Yaas, Boss, me do' op'n tuh de co't.

DETECTIVE: And yet you didn't see or hear anything?

PORGY: Uh yent shum, en' Uh yent yeddy'um. Uh bin eenside duh sleep en' me do' bin shet.

DETECTIVE: [*Exasperated*] : You're a damned liar. [*Turns away disgusted. Saunters toward door. To* POLICEMEN, *indicating* PETER]: He saw the killing. Take him along and lock him up as a material witness. [FIRST POLICEMAN *crosses to* PETER.]

FIRST POLICEMAN: [*Helping* PETER *to his feet*]: Come along, Uncle.

PETER: [*Shaking with terror*]: Uh yent nebbuh do'um, Boss!

POLICEMAN: Nobody says you did it. We're just taking you along as a witness.

[*But* PETER *does not understand.*]

SERENA: Wuh you gwi' do wid'um?

POLICEMAN: Lock him up. Come along. It ain't going to be so bad for you as for Crown, anyway.

SECOND POLICEMAN: [*To* DETECTIVE]: How about the cripple?

DETECTIVE [*Sourly*]: He couldn't have helped seeing it, but I can't make him come through. But it don't matter. One's enough to hang Crown [*with a short laugh*] — if we ever get him.

MARIA: [*To* FIRST POLICEMAN]: How long Petuh haffuh lock up?

FIRST POLICEMAN: Till we catch Crown.

PORGY: [*Sadly*]: Uh reckun Crown done loss 'ese'f een de palmettuh t'ickit, en' de rope ent bin mek wuh kin heng'um.

DETECTIVE: The the old man's out of luck. [*To* SERENA]: Remember! You've got to bury that nigger to-morrow or the Board of Health will take him and turn him over to the medical students.

PETER: Uh yent nebbuh do'um, boss!

DETECTIVE: [*To* FIRST POLICEMAN]: Come on! Get the old man in the wagon.

[PETER, *shaking in every limb, is led out. The* DETECTIVE *and* SECOND POLICEMAN *follow. A moment of desolated silence.*]

MARIA: Bline nigguh git 'long mo'bettuh een dis w'ull den dem wuh hab 'e two eye.

JAKE: Porgy ent hab much foot, 'cep'n' 'e sho hab onduhstan' fuh deal wid de buckruh.

PORGY: [*Slowly, as though half to himself*]: Uh sho' ent able fuh figguh dis t'ing out. Petuh bin uh good man, en' Crown ramify 'roun' en' kill Robbin. Now, Petuh lock-up lukkuh t'ief, en' Robbin dead wid 'e wife en' chillun lef' bidout dem farruh. Crown done git'way en' gwi' do de same t'ing 'gen.

[*The Negroes begin to sway and moan.*]

CLARA: Gone fuh true! Yaas, Jedus!

[*A voice raises the spiritual. It swells slowly. One voice joins in after another. The swaying and patting begin and grow slowly in tempo and emphasis. As before,* BESS *sways in silence.*]
"Wuh de mattuh, chillun?
Wuh de mattuh, chillun?
Wuh de mattuh, chillun?
You cyan' stan' still.

Pain hab de body.
Pain hab de body.
Pain hab de body.
En' Uh cyan' stan' still.

Wuh de mattuh, Sistuh?
Wuh de mattuh, Sistuh?
Wuh de mattuh, Sistuh
You cyan' stan' still?

Jedus hab we bredduh,
Jedus hab we bredduh,
Jedus hab we bredduh,
En' Uh cyan' stan' still."

[*The door opens and the* UNDERTAKER *bustles into the room with an air of great importance. He is a short, yellow Negro with a low, oily voice. He is dressed entirely in black. He crosses to* SERENA. *The song dies away, but the swaying continues to its rhythm.*]

UNDERTAKER: How de saucuh stan' me Sistuh? [*Glances appraisingly at saucer.*]

SERENA: [*In a flat, despairing voice*]: Dey ent but fuf'teen dolluh dey dey.

UNDERTAKER: Ummmm! Uh cyan' bury'um fuh fuf'teen dolluh.

JAKE: 'E haffuh bury tuhmorruh, eeduhso de Boa'd ub Hel't' gwi' g'em tuh de stoodun'.

SERENA: [*Wildly*]: Fuh Gawd sake bury'um een de grabeyaa'd! [*She rises to her knees and seizes the* UNDERTAKER'S *hand in both hers. Imploringly*]: Don' leh de stoodun' hab'um! Uh gwine wu'k Monday en' uh swaytogawd Uh gwi' pay eb'ry cent.

[*Even the swaying ceases now. The Negroes all wait tensely, their eyes riveted on the* UNDERTAKER'S *face, pleading silently. After a moment's hesitation, the* UNDERTAKER'S *professional manner slips from him.*]

UNDERTAKER: [*Simply*]: Berrywell, Sistuh. Wid de box en' one cyaaridge, 'e gwi' cos' me mo'nuh twenty-fibe. But Uh gwi' he'p you t'ru. [*An expression of vast relief sweeps into every face.* SERENA *silently relaxes across the foot of the bed, her head between her outstretched arms.*] You kin git ready uhlly tuhmorruh? 'E uh long way tuh de grabeyaa'd.

[*The* UNDERTAKER *goes out door. The Negroes gaze silently after him with eyes filled with gratitude. There is a moment of silence after his departure. Then, carried out of herself by sympathy and gratitude,* BESS, *forgetful of the ban laid upon her, lifts her strong, beautiful voice triumphantly.*]

BESS: "Oh, Uh hab uh leetle bredduh een de new grabeyaa'd wuh outshine de sun, outshine de sun,"
[PORGY'S *voice joins hers*]: "Outshine de sun."

[*By the fourth line, many of the Negro voices have joined in, and the song grows steadily in volume and fervour.*] "Oh, Uh hab uh leetle bredduh een de new grabeyaa'd wuh outshine de sun. En' Uh gwi' meet'um een de Prommus Lan'."

[BESS'S *voice is heard again for one brief moment alone as it rises high and clear on the first line of the chorus*]: "Uh gwi' meet'um een de Prommus Lan'!"

[*Then a full chorus, with deep basses predominating, crashes in on the second line of the refrain.* SERENA, *last of all, joins enthusiastically in the chorus.*]

"Oh, Uh gwi' meet'um een de Prommus Lan'!
Uh gwi' meet'um, meet'um, meet'um,
Uh gwi' meet'um, meet'um, meet'um,
Uh gwi' meet'um een de Prommus Lan'!

Oh, Uh hab uh manshun up on high
Wuh ent mek wid han',
Ent mek wid han',
Ent mek wid han',
Oh, Uh hab uh manshun up on high
Wuh ent mek wid han',
En' Uh gwi' meet'um een de Prommus Lan'!"

[*The beautiful old spiritual beats triumphantly through the narrow room, steadily gaining in speed.*

SERENA *ıs the first to leap to her feet and begin to "shout." One by one, as the spirit moves them, the Negroes follow her example till they are all on their feet, swaying, shuffling, clapping their hands.*

BESS *leads the "shouting" as she has the singing, throwing her whole soul into an intricate shuffle and complete turn. Each Negro "shouts" in his own individual way, some dancing in place, others merely swaying and patting their hands. "Hallylooyuh" and cries of 'Yaas, Lawd" are interjected into the singing. And the rhythm swells till the old walls seem to rock and surge with the sweep of it.*]

CURTAIN

"Shouting" is the term given by the Carolina Negroes to the body rhythms and steps with which they accompany their emotional songs.

ACT TWO

ACT TWO

Scene One

St. Michael's chimes the quarters and strikes one. Morning.

The court is full of movement, the Negroes going about their tasks. At right front, a group of fishermen are rigging their lines. They are working leisurely with much noisy laughter and banter. Occasionally, a snatch of song is heard.

PORGY *is sitting at his window. The soap-box car stands by his door, the goat is inside the room. Occasionally looks out door.*

JAKE: De fish duh run good dese day out pass de baar.

MINGO: [*An onlooker*]: Uh yeddy suh de Beefu't mens git summuch'uh fish yistiddy, de boat flo' stan' lukkuh 'e mek ub silbuh.

JIM: Uh yeddy dem haffuh t'row back half de ketch. Dey hab tummuch fuh de maa'kut.

JAKE: Yaas, suh de fish duh run, en' us bes' fish w'ile dey duh run good.

JIM: Fuh true! Septembuh storm gwi' come soon, en' fish ent lub eas' win' en' muddy watuh.

ANNIE: [*Calling across court*]: Oonuh mus'e fuhgit 'bout de picnic! De perrade gwi'staa't soon!

MINGO: Sho' 'nuf, Sistuh!
[*The men begin to gather up their fishing gear.*]

PORGY: [*At window. Solicitously*]: Bess, you sho' you ent wan' gone tuh de picnic? You know Porgy uh good-stand'n' membuh ub "De Son en' Daa'tuh ub Repent Ye Suh de Lawd."

BESS: [*Unseen within room*]: Uh rudduh stay home wid you.

PORGY: You hab right fuh gone, same lukkuh eb'ry odduh 'ooman een Catfish Row.

BESS: [*In unconvincing voice*]: Uh yent cyah much 'bout no picnic.

[PORGY *is troubled. Sits in silence.*]

SPORTING LIFE: [*Who has sauntered over to group of fishermen*]: Oonuh mens gwine de picnic?

JAKE: 'Co'se us gwine! Mek you t'ink us ent gwine?

SPORTING LIFE: Uh jis' duh ax. No picnic bin hab tuh New Yawk. You still hab de picnic tuh Kittywah?

JIM: Liss'n tuh Spo't'n' Life! 'E done bin New Yawk fuh six munt', en' 'e ax ef us still hab picnic tuh Kittywah!

[*They laugh.*]

[SPORTING LIFE *moves off. Sits at* MARIA'S *table.* LILY *joins the group of men.*]

JAKE: Berrywellden, mens, Uh ready fuh ride luck faar ez 'e gwine! 'Fo' dayclean tuhmorruh us gwi' push de Sea Gull spang Blackfish Bank 'fo' us drap ankuh. Uh figguh de boat gwi' full tuh 'e gonnil wid de pyo' fish w'en us git back.

LILY: Oonuh gwi' tek de Sea Gull out pass de baar? [*She laughs. Calls out to* NELSON, *who is on far side of court*]: Nelson, you yeddy? De mens aim fuh tek de Sea Gull tuh Blackfish Bank! [NELSON *joins the group.* CLARA, *overhearing, slowly approaches, her baby in her arms.* LILY *turns to the others.*] Oonuh bes' keep you ole washtub close

tuh home. Wait 'tell you git uh good boat lukkuh de Muskittuh 'fo' you trabble.

[*All the men and* LILY *laugh delightedly.*]

JAKE: Muskittuh bawn een de watuh. Stillyet 'e kin drowndid.

[*All laugh,* LILY *slapping* NELSON'S *shoulder in her appreciation.*
CLARA *has stood silently beside them with anxious eyes.*]

CLARA: Jake! You plan fuh tek de Sea Gull tuh Blackfish Bank?
Ent you know 'e time fuh Septembuh storm?

JAKE: [*Laughing reassuringly*]: You 'membuh us hab storm las'
yeah, enty? Storm ent come two yeah han' runn'n'!

CLARA: Jake, Uh yent wan' you fuh gone pass de baar!

JAKE: How you figguh us gwi' pay fuh we man-chile eddycashun?

[*They all laugh, except* CLARA.]

CLARA: Dey odduh way fuh mek money 'side fish.

JAKE: Yeddy de 'ooman! Mebbe you wan' me fuh swing cott'n
bale!

[*The men laugh.*

SCIPIO *is playing about the court with a broad red sash pinned
across his breast from shoulder to waist. It bears the legend,
"Repent Ye Saith the Lord." From the boy's breast flutters a
yellow ribbon with the word "Marshal." He struts about
court leading an imaginary parade.* JAKE, *looking about for
change of subject, sees* SCIPIO *and starts to his feet.*] Yuh,
Scipio! Who sash you got? [SCIPIO *backs away.* JAKE *pur-
sues.*] Come'yuh! Dat me sash! G'em yuh!

[*Not watching where he is going,* SCIPIO, *in his flight from* JAKE,
runs straight into MARIA, *who delivers him to* JAKE.]

MARIA: Yuh 'e yiz, Jake!

JAKE: T'engk you, Sistuh. [*To* SCIPIO, *while he rescues his sash and badge*]: How you t'ink Uh gwi' lead dis perrade ef you ractify me sash? [*Pins ribbons on his own breast. Sits on washing bench. Lights pipe.*]

[*The crowd begins to break up with noisy laughter and joking.*

SERENA *comes in at gate, wearing a neat white apron and a hat. Crosses to* PORGY'S *door, greeting her friends as she passes them.*]

SERENA: [*To the men*]: 'E uh fine day fuh picnic!

JIM: 'E yiz, fuh true, Sistuh!

[SERENA *knocks at* PORGY'S *door.* BESS *opens it.* SERENA *pays no attention to her.*]

SERENA: [*Looking through* BESS]: Porgy! [*Sees him at window. Crosses to him.*] Dey you iz. Uh hab good news. Uh done bin tuh see me w'ite folk 'bout Petuh.

PORGY: Wuh dey suh?

SERENA: Dey suh dey hab w'ite juntlemun fr'en' name Mistuh Aa'chdale. 'E uh law man en' 'e kin git Petuh out. Uh tell'um you de one fuh talk tuhr'um, 'kase you hab onduhstan' fuh talk tuh buckruh. Dey suh 'e gwi' come fuh see you, sence you cripple en' 'e come dis side eb'ry day. [*Turns away, ignoring* BESS. *Crosses, sits beside* JAKE, *takes out and lights her pipe.*]

[MARIA *is serving a late breakfast to* SPORTING LIFE. JIM *and* MINGO *have joined him at table. St. Michael's chimes the quarter hour.* MARIA *crosses to pump to fill kettle. After a few puffs,* SERENA *whispers loudly to* JAKE]: 'E uh shame w'en uh good Gawd-fayr'n' 'ooman haffuh lib 'neet de same roof wid uh she-debble lukkuh Crown Bess.

JAKE: 'E yent seem luk 'e haa'm nobody, en' Porgy seem

lukkuh 'e wan'um 'roun'.

MARIA: Porgy done change sence dat 'ooman come fuh lib wid'um.

SERENA: How dat 'e change?

MARIA: Uh tell you dat nigguh happy, fuh true.

SERENA: Dat 'ooman ent de kin' fuh mek cripple happy. 'E tek man lukkuh Crown fuh hol'um down.

MARIA: Mebbe so, 'cep' Porgy ent know dat yet. En' ef uh man de kin' wuh need 'ooman, 'e gwi' call 'ese'f happy same so.

JAKE: Dat de trute! De man gwi' tie up 'e eye 'long de 'ooman 'tell de 'ooman stan' same lukkuh de Queen ub Shebuh.

MARIA: Porgy duh t'ink 'e hab uh she-Gawd een 'e room.

SERENA: Dey all kind'uh Gawd, en' Porgy hab de kin' wuh gwi' g'em Hell. Uh lub Porgy, 'cep' Uh yent gwi' gib' Bess de time ub day.

MARIA: Mebbe so, Sistuh. But watch Porgy! 'E nyusetuh hate all de chillun, 'cep' now w'en 'e come home 'e hab candy ball fuhr'um.

JAKE: Uh tell you dat 'ooman ———

[BESS *crosses to pump with bucket.*]

SERENA: [*The three are silent watching* BESS. *She is neatly dressed, walks with queenly dignity, passes them as though they did not exist, fills her bucket, swings it easily to her head, turns from them with an air of cool scorn, and recrosses to her own door. The three look after her with varying expressions:* MARIA *interested,* SERENA *indignant,* JAKE *admiring.*]

JAKE: Fuh sho' 'e yent ax none 'e navuh fuh wissit'um!

SERENA: You po' chupit nigguh! You ent shame fuh set dey 'fo' me en' talk sweet-mout' talk 'bout dat debble'ub'uh Bess? [*Making eyes at him*]: Ef Uh binnuh man, Uh duh sabe me sweet-mout' talk fuh uh good 'ooman.

JAKE: Ef you binnuh man — [*Pauses, looking thoughtfully at her, then shakes his head.*] Ent no use. You cyan' onduhstan'. Dat sump'n' freemale ent know nutt'n' 'bout. [*Knocks ashes from his pipe.*]

[MARIA *has turned toward her table. She suddenly puts down her kettle, strides to the table, seizes* SPORTING LIFE'S *hand, opens the fingers before he has time to resist, and blows a white powder from his palm.*]

SPORTING LIFE: [*Furiously*]: Wuh you t'ink you duh do! Dat stuff cos' money! [MARIA *stands back, arms akimbo, staring down at him for a moment of silence.* SPORTING LIFE *shifts uneasily in his chair.*]

MARIA: [*In stentorian tones*]: Nigguh, Uh duh figguh ef 'e mo' bettuh ef Uh kill you deestunt 'long you fr'en', eeduhso lef' you fuh de buckruh heng? Uh yent say nutt'n' w'en you git dese boy drunk-up wid you rot-gut likkuh, but nobody ent gwi' sell no happy dus' 'roun' dis shop! You yeddy wuh duh suh?

SPORTING LIFE: Come on, ole lady. Don' talk lukkuh dese ole kyarrysene 'il lamp nigguh. Up tuh New Yawk, weh Uh binnuh wait een uh bo'd'n'-house ——-

MARIA: Bo'd'n'-house! You figguh dese gal you try fuh tek wid you tuh New Yawk gwi' lib tuh bo'd'n'-house?

MARIA: [*Shouting*]: Don' you onrabble you mout' 'bout New Yawk 'roun' yuh! Uh berry lub fuh gone down tuh dat New Yawk boat, en' tek eb'ry Gawd nigguh wuh come up de gangplank wid 'e Josuf coat 'pun 'e back, en' uh glass headlight 'pun 'e buzzum en' drap'um tuh de catfish 'fo' 'e foot hab chance tuh hit deestunt groun'. Me belly done full'up wid New Yawk talk! [*Bangs table so violently with her fist that* SPORTING LIFE *leaps from his chair and extends a propitiating hand toward her.*]

SPORTING LIFE: 'E stan' so, Sistuh! Come leh we be fr'en'!

MARIA: Fr'en' wid you? One dese day mebbe Uh gwi' leddown wid rattlesnake, en' w'en dat day come, you kin come 'long en' git een de bed. 'Tell dat day come, keep you no'count cawcus een New Yawk 'tell de debble ready fuh tek chaa'ge obuhr'um.

[SIMON FRAZIER, *an elderly Negro dressed in black frock coat, comes in at the gate, looks about, crosses to* MARIA'S *table.* MARIA *is still glaring at* SPORTING LIFE *so ferociously that* FRAZIER *hesitates.* MARIA *looks up and sees him. She is suddenly all smiles.*]

MARIA: Mawnin', lawyuh. You duh look fuh somebody?

FRAZIER: Porgy lib yuh, enty?

MARIA: 'E yiz, fuh true. 'E room obuh yanduh.

FRAZIER: T'engk you, Sistuh. [*Crosses toward* PORGY'S *door.*]

LILY: [*Who is near* PORGY'S *door*]: Porgy! Lawyuh Fra'juh come fuh see you!

[MARIA *gives* SPORTING LIFE *final glare and enters shop.* BESS *helps* PORGY *on to doorstep and returns to room.*]

FRAZIER: Mawnin', Porgy!

PORGY: Mawnin', lawyuh!

FRAZIER: Uh come fuh see you 'bout some buckruh bidness.

PORGY: Huh?

FRAZIER: Uh binnuh talk wid Mistuh Alan Aa'chdale yistiddy en' 'e gib me metsidge fuh you.

PORGY: Who 'e yiz?

FRAZIER: [*In disgust*]: Who 'e yiz? You ent know Mistuh Alan Aa'chdale. Me en' him alltwo iz lawyuh.

PORGY: [*Uneasily*]: Wuh 'e wan' wid me?

FRAZIER: Uh bin fuh shum 'bout pribate bidness, en' 'e ax'me, "Mistuh Fra'juh, you know dat black scoundul wuh hitch 'e goat 'neet' me winduh eb'ry mawnin'?" Uh telll'um, "Yaas, Mistuh Aa'chdale, Uh know'um." En' 'e say, "Well, w'en you gone out, tell'um mus' moobe on." W'en Uh gone out, you ent dey dey, so Uh come fuh tell you mus' moobe on.

PORGY: Mek 'e yent tell me 'ese'f?

FRAZIER: You t'ink Mistuh Aa'chdale hab time fuh talk tuh nigguh? No, suh! 'E pit de case een me han', en' 'e gimme t'oruhty fuh tell you mus' fin' anudduh place fuh hitch.

PORGY: [*Unhappily*]: Uh binnuh hitch tuh dat cawnuh mos' uh munt', now. Mek 'e yent wan' me fuh hitch dey dey?

FRAZIER: [*Scratching his head*]: Uh yent know, fuh sho'. 'E say sump'n' 'bout de goat en' de cummodity wuh abbuhtize on de chaa'yut. [*Pointing to cart*]: Pyo' en' f'aygrunt. Dat de soap, enty? Uh figguh Mistuh Aa'chdale t'ink you goat need soap.

PORGY: [*Astonished*]: Wuh uh goat gwi' do wid soap?

FRAZIER: [*Also puzzled*]: Uh yent puhzac'ly know! [BESS *comes to doorway and stands behind* PORGY. FRAZIER *resumes his authoritative tone.*] But Uh know you hab tuh moobe on. [FRAZIER *looks up and sees* BESS]: How you do? [*Looks at her, scrutinizing.*] You Crown Bess, enty?

PORGY: No, suh 'e yent! 'E Porgy Bess!

FRAZIER: [*Sensing business*]: Fuh true? Den you gwi' need uh deewo'se.

PORGY: Wuh dat iz?

FRAZIER: Ef de 'ooman gwi' lib wid you, 'e haffuh hab deewo'se f'um Crown eeduhso 'e yent legal. [*Takes legal-looking document from pocket. Shows it to* PORGY. PORGY *looks at it, much impressed. Passes it to* BESS.]

PORGY: Hummuch 'e cos'?

FRAZIER: One dolluh, ef 'e yent hab tail tie 'puntop'um. [PORGY *looks dubious.* FRAZIER *quickly takes huge seal from his coat-tail pocket. Shows it to* PORGY.]

FRAZIER: W'en you git deewo'se, Uh seal'um fuh sho' you done pay cash fuhr'um.

PORGY: Bess, you wan' deewo'se, enty?

BESS: [*With longing*]: Wuh you t'ink, Porgy?
[*The other Negroes are gradually edging nearer to listen.*]

PORGY: Uh gwi' buy you deewo'se. Fetch me hengkitchuh wid me money een'um. [BESS *goes into room and returns immediately with a number of small coins tied up in a rag, hands it to* PORGY. *He laboriously counts out a dollar in nickels and pennies. In the meantime,* FRAZIER *is filling in document with fountain pen. Group of Negroes now listening frankly.* FRAZIER *takes coins from* PORGY. *Counts them.* BESS *holds out her hand for document.*]

FRAZIER: [*Pocketing coins*]: Hol'on! 'E yent lawful yet! [*Holding paper in hands, lowers glasses on his nose. Begins in solemn tones*]: Wuh you name iz?

BESS: Bess. [FRAZIER *makes note.*]

FRAZIER: How ole you iz?

BESS: Uh een me twenty-six yeah.

FRAZIER: You wan' deewo'se f'um dis man, Crown?

BESS: Yaas, boss.

FRAZIER: 'Dress de co't, "You Onnuh".

BESS: Yaas, You Onnuh.

FRAZIER: W'en you en' Crown marri'd? [BESS *hesitates*.]

BESS: Uh yent rightly 'membuh, boss ——- You Onnuh.

FRAZIER: One yeah? Ten yeah?

BESS: Uh done tell you, Uh yent 'membuh!

LILY: Dey ent nebbuh bin marri'd.

FRAZIER: [*To* BESS]: Dat de trute?

BESS: Yaas, You Onnuh.

FRAZIER: [*Triumphantly*]: Den de deewo'se hab tail tie 'punto-p'um.

BESS: Uh yent know dat mattuh!

PORGY: Ef you cyan' ontie de tail, gimme back me dolluh.

FRAZIER: Whodat say Uh cyan' ontie de tail? 'Cep' deewo'se wid tail gwi' cos' two dolluh. 'E tek uh berry soon-man fuh deewo'se 'ooman wuh yent marri'd.

BESS: Don' you pay'um no two dolluh, Porgy. 'E yent wut' no two dolluh.

FRAZIER: Berrywellden! Ef you wan' lib een sin. [*Takes coins from pocket and begins to count. Seeing that they do not weaken, he pauses abruptly in his counting.*] Sence us ole fr'en', Uh gwi' mek dis deewo'se one dolluh en' fufty cent. [*Again takes out impressive seal.* PORGY *eyes seal, greatly*

impressed. Begins counting out more pennies. FRAZIER
affixes seal. Hands it to PORGY. *Pockets extra money.*]

FRAZIER: 'E yent cos dat much, w'en one dolluh en' fufty cent
kin change you f'um uh 'ooman tuh uh lady.

BESS: [*Happily*]: T'engk you berry much, You Onnuh!

FRAZIER: Glad fuh saa'b you. Lemme know w'en you ready fuh
buy marri'd license.

PORGY: Wuffuh 'e need marri'd license? 'E done habe
deewo'se, enty?

FRAZIER: Attuh deewo'se you need marri'd license — dat iz, ef
you wan' lib stylish lukkuh de buckruh. [PORGY *and* BESS
look quite depressed at prospect of further complications.]
Well, good-mawnin', Mis' Porgy. [*Turns to go. To*
MARIA]: You hab some coffee fuh tas'e me mout'?

MARIA: Uh hab, fuh true. Step right obuh yuh. [*She and* FRA-
ZIER *enter cookshop. The court is alive with noisy laughter
and action. A fish vendor is calling his wares. St. Michael's
is chiming the half hour.* MARIA *is bustling back and forth
serving the men at her table.* SERENA *is pumping water and
calling to her friends.* ANNIE *is holding* CLARA'S *baby, rocking and tossing it.* CLARA *is rearranging sash with motto
"Repent Ye Saith the Lord" across* JAKE'S *breast, and con-
sulting the others as to the proper angle. The sash adjusted,*
JAKE *bursts into song. "Buh Rabbit, wuh you duh do dey!"*
LILY *answers with second line of song. The duet continues.*
SCIPIO *runs in at gate. Runs to* SERENA.]

SCIPIO: Uh buckruh duh come'yuh! Uh yeddy'um ax ef dis
Catfish Row.

[*The Negroes suddenly break off in their tasks.* JAKE *ceases to
sing.*]

NELSON: [*Calling to* SERENA]: Wuh 'e suh?

SERENA: [*In guarded voice, but addressing the court in general*]: W'ite juntlemun!

[*There is a deep silence, contrasting strangely with noise and movement that preceded it.* ANNIE *gives* CLARA *her baby, goes quickly inside her own door.* JAKE *removes sash, puts it in pocket.* SERENA *retreats behind her tubs. The men at table give absorbed attention to their food.* MARIA *serves them in silence without looking up.* SCIPIO *becomes engrossed in tinkering with an old barrel hoop.* BESS *goes inside.* PORGY *feigns sleep.*

ALAN ARCHDALE, *a tall, kindly man in early middle age, whose bearing at once stamps him the aristocrat, enters the court, looks about at the Negroes, all ostensibly oblivious of his presence.*]

ARCHDALE: [*Calling to* SCIPIO]: Boy! [SCIPIO *approaches, reluctant, shuffling.*] I'm looking for a man by the name of Porgy. Which is his room? [SCIPIO *shuffles and is silent.*] Don't you know Porgy?

SCIPIO: [*His eyes on the ground*]: No, suh!

ARCHDALE: He lives here, doesn't he?

SCIPIO: Uh yent know, boss!

[CLARA *is nearest.* ARCHDALE *crosses to her. She listens submissively, her eyes lowered.*]

ARCHDALE: I'm looking for a man named Porgy. Can you direct me to his room?

CLARA: [*Polite, but utterly negative*]: Porgy? [*Repeats the name slowly as though trying to remember.*] No, boss, Uh nebbuh yeddy 'bout nobody 'roun' yuh name Porgy.

ARCHDALE: Come, you must know him. I am sure he lives in Catfish Row.

CLARA: [*Raising her voice*]: Ennybody know uh man name Porgy?

[*Several of the Negroes repeat the name to one another, with shakes of their heads.*]

ARCHDALE: [*Laughing reassuringly*]: I'm a friend of his, Mr. Alan Archdale, and I want to help him.

[SERENA *approaches. Looks keenly at* ARCHDALE.]

SERENA: Go 'long en' wake Porgy up! Cyan' you tell we people w'en you shum?

[*A light of understanding breaks over* CLARA'S *face.*]

CLARA: Oh, you mean Porgy? Uh yent onduhstan' wuh name you duh call!

[*Voices all about the court:* Oh, de juntlemun mean Porgy! Mek we yent onduhstan'? CLARA *crosses to* PORGY'S *door, all smiles.*] Juntlemun come fuh see Porgy!

[PORGY *appears to wake.* ARCHDALE *crosses to him.*]

PORGY: How you do, boss?

ARCHDALE: You're Porgy? Oh, you're the fellow who rides in the goat cart. [*Sits on step.*]

PORGY: Yaas, boss, Uh hab goat.

ARCHDALE: Tell me about your friend who got locked up on account of the Robbins murder.

PORGY: [*His face inscrutable*]: W'ymek'so you wan' know, boss?

ARCHDALE: Why, I'm the Rutledge's lawyer, and I look after their coloured folks for them. Serena Robbins is the daughter of their old coachman, and she asked them to help out her friend.

PORGY: [*A shade of suspicion still in his voice*]: Petuh ent hab no money, boss, en' Uh jis' duh baig f'um do' tuh do'.

ARCHDALE: [*Reassuringly*]: It will not take any money. At least, not much. And I am sure that Mrs. Rutledge will take care of that. So you can go right ahead and tell me all about it.

[PORGY'S *suspicions vanish.*]

PORGY: Dis how 'e bin, boss. Crown kill Robbin, en' Petuh shum. Crown done git'way, en' dey done lock up ole Petuh.

ARCHDALE: I see, as a witness.

PORGY: Ontel dey ketch Crown. But ef dey keep'um 'tell den, dat ole man done lock up fuh life.

ARCHDALE: [*Under his breath*]: The dirty hounds! [*He is silent for a moment, his face set and stern.* PORGY *waits.* ARCHDALE *turns wearily to him.*] Of course, we can go to law about this, but it will take no end of time. There is an easier way.

[*Across the sunlit walls of Catfish Row falls the shadow of a great bird flying low, evidently just out of range of vision of audience. There is a sudden great commotion in the court. Cries of* "Dribe'um off, Bess! Don' leh'um light! *Brooms are waved at the bird overhead. Bricks thrown.* PORGY *looks up in anxiety.* BESS *comes to door with broom.* ARCHDALE *rises in perplexity.*]

PORGY: Dribe'um off, Bess! Don' leh'um light.

ARCHDALE: What is it? What's the matter? [*The shadow rises high. The commotion dies down.*]

PORGY: Dat uh buzzut! You ent know buzzut eat dead people en' t'ing?

ARCHDALE: But there's no one dead here, is there?

PORGY: Boss, dat bu'd mean trubble! W'en uh buzzut fol' 'e wing en' light obuh you do', you ent gwi' nebbuh happy no mo'.

[*With relief, the Negroes stand watching the bird disappear in the distance.* ARCHDALE *also looks after it.*]

SERENA: [*Leaning from her window and surveying court*]: Uh too shame fuh shum all dese chupit nigguh sho' out 'fo' w'ite juntlemun. Dat buzzut seddown 'puntop Maria table day 'fo' yistiddy. All ub we shum! En' nobody ent hab no bad luck.

MARIA: [*Indignantly*]: Bad luck! Wuh dat 'ooman call bad luck? Uh hab 'nuf drunk mens come'yuh fuh eat yistiddy. En' dey mos' ractify me shop, enty? [*Goes into shop muttering indignantly.*]

ARCHDALE: [*Turning back to* PORGY]: Now, listen. Peter must have someone to go his bond. Do you know a man by the name of Huysenberg who keeps a corner shop over by the East End wharf?

PORGY: [*His face darkening*]: Yaas, suh, Uh know'um. 'E rob eb'ry nigguh 'e git 'e han' on.

ARCHDALE: I see you know him. Well, take him this ten dollars and tell him that you want him to go Peter's bond. He hasn't any money of his own, and his shop is in his wife's name, but he has an arrangement with the magistrate that makes him entirely satisfactory. [*Hands* PORGY *a ten-dollar bill.*] Do you understand?

PORGY: Yaas, boss. T'engk you, boss.

[ARCHDALE, *about to go, hesitates, looks at goat-cart.*]

ARCHDALE: Porgy, there's another little matter I want to speak
to you about. The last few weeks you've been begging right
under my office window. I wish you'd find another place.
[*Noticing* PORGY'S *troubled expression*]: There are lots of
other street corners.

PORGY: [*Sadly*]: Uh done try all de odduh cawnuh, boss. Eb'ry
time Uh stop, somebody tell me mus' moobe on. Uh bin
'neet' you winduh de t'ree munt' done gone, en' Uh figguh, "Porgy, you fix fuh life. You done fin' uh juntlemun
wuh hab place een 'e haa't fuh po' cripple."

ARCHDALE: I have a place in my heart for the cripple but not for
the goat.

PORGY: Dis uh berry mannussubble goat, boss. Lawyuh Fra'juh
say you t'ink 'e need soap. Uh cyan' figguh huccome 'e
need soap. Dis week mek de two week, han' runn'n' dat
goat nyam all Serena wash soap.

ARCHDALE: He doesn't need it inside.

PORGY: [*Mystified*]: Wuh goat gwi' do wid soap outside? [*Suddenly enlightened*]: Oh, you ent luk how 'e smell? [FRAZIER
comes from shop. Sees ARCHDALE. *Approaches. Stands waiting, hat in hand.* PORGY *is now all smiles.*] Berry well,
boss. 'Fo' tuhmurruh Uh gwi' hab dis goat so wash, 'e gwi'
smell lukkuh rose f'um de paa'k.

ARCHDALE: I'm sorry, Porgy. But you must find another place.

FRAZIER: Mawnin', Mistuh Aa'chdale. Uh done gib' dis nigguh
you metsidge. [*Sternly to* PORGY]: 'Membuh wuh Uh tell
you! You haffuh moobe on!

ARCHDALE: All right, Frazier. [*To* PORGY]: If Peter isn't out in
a week, let me know. [*Turning to take leave*]: I suppose
you're all going to the picnic to-day.

[*The Negroes nod and smile.* PORGY *looks wistfully at* BESS, *who stands behind him in the doorway.* ARCHDALE *is crossing toward gate.*]

JAKE: Yaas, boss. Us gwine!

PORGY: Bess, you ent change you min' 'bout de picnic now, sence you hab deewo'se?

[ARCHDALE *catches word "divorce," turns.*]

ARCHDALE: Divorce?

PORGY: [*Proudly*]: Yaas, boss. Mistuh Fra'juh sell me 'ooman uh deewo'se. 'E uh onnuhrubble 'ooman, now.

ARCHDALE: [*Sternly, to* FRAZIER, *who is looking guilty*]: Didn't the judge tell you that if you sold any more divorces he'd put you in jail? I've a good mind to report you.

FRAZIER: Dat jedge mus'e fuhgit Uh yiz uh Dimmycrack!

ARCHDALE: That won't help you now. The gentleman from the North, who has come down to better moral conditions among the Negroes, says you are a menace to morals. He's going to have you indicted if you don't quit.

PORGY: [*Suspiciously; handing paper to Archdale*]: Dis ent no gook luk 'e stan', boss? 'Kase Uh cyan' pay fuh no mo' 'tailmunt. [*As* ARCHDALE *glances over the paper,* PORGY *glares vindictively at* FRAZIER.] Dat nigguh come'long een 'e By-Gawd coat, en' 'fo' you hab time fuh crack you teet', 'e done gone wid you las' cent.

ARCHDALE: [*Reading*]: "I, Simon Frazier, hereby divorce Bess and Crown for a charge of one dollar and fifty cents cash. Signed, SIMON FRAZIER." Well, that's simple enough. [*Examines seal.*] "Sealed — Charleston Steamboat Company." Where did you get this seal?

FRAZIER: Uh buy'um f'um de Jew junk shop, boss.

ARCHDALE: Don't you know that there is no such thing as divorce in this state?

FRAZIER: Uh yeddy dey ent no shisuh t'ing fuh de buckruh; but de nigguh need'um dat bad, Uh yent see wuffuh Uh cyan' g'em deewo'se fuh sattify'um. [*His voice breaks.*] Dem deewo'se me libb'n', boss, en' dey keep de nigguh skrate, alltwo.

ARCHDALE: How's that?

FRAZIER: De jedge say dey hab tuh lib tuhgedduh ontel dey done fuh dead. 'Cep'n' nigguh mek ent so. Uh done git de nigguh moralize, en' now 'e say 'e gwi' pit me een de jail ef Uh yent stop. Stillyet, de nigguh gwi' lef' onenurruh. Ef 'e yent cos' de nigguh nutt'n' fuh lef' 'e wife, 'e ent gwi' stay wid'um mo'nuh munt'. W'en 'e haffuh pay uh dolluh fuh lef'um, 'e gwi' stay mo'longuh 'fo' 'e trabble.

[ARCHDALE *keeps from laughing with difficulty.*]

BESS: Me deewo'se cyan' specify, boss? Porgy done pay one dolluh en' fufty cent fuhr'um.

ARCHDALE: [*Looking at paper*]: I could hardly say that it is legal.

BESS: Dat mean 'e kin specify?

ARCHDALE: Well, sometimes.

PORGY: 'Nuf we fr'en' hab deewo'se, boss.

ARCHDALE: [*With accusing look at* FRAZIER, *who cringes*]: So I hear. [*Again consults paper.*]: You've left this man, Crown, and intend to stay with Porgy?

BESS: Yaas'suh, boss!

ARCHDALE: I suppose this makes a respectable woman of you. Um — on the whole — I'd keep it. I imagine that respectability at one-fifty would be a bargain anywhere. [*Hands paper to* BESS. *Turns back to* FRAZIER.] But remember, Frazier: *No more divorces!* Or to jail you go. I won't report you this time. [*The goat sticks its head out door.* PORGY *throws his arm around its neck.* ARCHDALE *turns to go.*] Good morning. [*Crosses to gate.*]

FRAZIER: [*Close by* PORGY'S *door. Recovering from his emotion enough to speak*]: Gawd bress you, boss! Good mawnin', suh.

PORGY: [*Imitating* FRAZIER'S *professional manner*]: Moobe on, please! Uh hab uh puhlite goat wuh ent lub fuh smell jail bu'd. [ARCHDALE, *overhearing, laughs suddenly. Goes out gate, his shoulders shaking with laughter.* FRAZIER *moves off, talks to Negroes in background, and soon leaves the court.* BESS *sits by* PORGY *on step.*] You yeddy de boss laugh, enty?

BESS: Uh yeddy'um laugh, fuh true!

PORGY: [*Hugging goat*]: No, no, bubbuh, us ent gwi' moobe on. W'en nigguh mek buckruh laugh, 'e done win. Us gwi' spen' we life 'neet' Mistuh Aa'chdale winduh. You watch!

[*Draws himself up by door frame, goes inside.* BESS *remains on step. St. Michael's chimes the three-quarter hour. Preparations for the picnic are now at their height. One by one the women, when not on stage, have changed to their most gorgeously coloured dresses. Men and women are now wearing sashes all bearing the legend: "Repent Ye Saith the Lord." The leaders have also badges denoting their various ranks: "Marshal," etc. Baskets are being assembled in the court. The court is full of bustle and confusion.* SPORTING LIFE *saunters over to* BESS, *who is sitting on step wistfully watching the picnic preparations.*]

SPORTING LIFE: 'Lo, Bess, gwine tuh de picnic?

BESS: No, Uh reckun Uh gwi' stay home.

SPORTING LIFE: Picnic awright fuh small-town nigguh, but us lub de high-life. Uh cyan' figguh w'y'mek you duh heng 'roun' yuh. Wid you looks, en' you way wid mens, us kin mek big money tuh New Yawk.

BESS: [*Quietly*]: Uh yent nebbuh see uh nigguh mo' ondeestunt en' no'count den you!

SPORTING LIFE: [*Laughing*]: Oh, come on! How 'bout uh leetle tetch ub happy dus', jis' fuh ole time?

BESS: Uh done t'ru wid happy dus'!

SPORTING LIFE: Come on! Gimme you han'. [*Reaches out and takes her hand, draws it toward him, and with other hand unfolds paper ready to pour powder.*]

BESS: [*Wavering*]: Uh tell you Uh t'ru!

SPORTING LIFE: Jis' uh pinch. Ent 'nuf tuh hu't uh flea.

[BESS *snatches her hand away.*]

BESS: Uh done gitt'ru wid happy dus'!

SPORTING LIFE: Uh yent b'leebe dat. Nobody ebbuh gitt'ru wid happy dus'. [*Again he takes her hand and she does not resist. Gazes fascinated at the powder.* PORGY'S *hand reaches suddenly into the open space of the door; seizes* SPORTING LIFE'S *wrist in an iron grip.* SPORTING LIFE *looks at the hand in astonishment mixed with a sort of horror.*] Leggo, you dam' cripple! [*The hand twists* SPORTING LIFE'S *wrist till he relinquishes* BESS'S *hand and grunts with pain. Then* PORGY'S *hand is silently withdrawn.*] Gawd 'e hab strengk fuh uh piece ub man!

BESS: [*Rising*]: Go'way, now!

SPORTING LIFE: [*Regaining his swagger*]: Awright, you mens

kin come en' go, but ole Spo't'n' Life en' happy dus' ent
gwine no weh! [*Saunters along — goes out gate.*]

[*From the distance is heard the blare of a discordant band. It is
playing* "Ent It Haa'd tuh Be uh Nigguh," *though the tune is
scarcely recognizable to the audience. The Negroes, however,
are untroubled by the discords. One or another sings a line or
two of the song. A jumble of voices rises above the
music:* "Yuh come de offun!" "Dey de offun ban' down de
block!" "Leh we go!" *etc. A man passes outside the gate,
stopping long enough to call in to the occupants of Catfish
Row:* "Eb'rybody een line up de block. You nigguh bes'
mek'ace! PORGY *comes out on doorstep to watch. Sits.* BESS
stands beside him absorbed in the gay scene. PORGY *looks at
her keenly, troubled.*]

JAKE: [*In the midst of his preparations*]: Come 'long tuh de
picnic, Bess!

PORGY: [*Triumphantly*]: Go 'long, Bess! Ent you yeddy Jake
ax you fuh gone 'long?

BESS: 'Nuf mens ax'me. You ent yeddy none de lady say
nutt'n'!

PORGY: Bess, you kin pit on me laa'ge sash en' be jis' as good
ez enny 'ooman dey dey.

BESS: [*With a little laugh*]: You en' me bofe know 'e gwi' tek
mo'nuh sash.

[*The confusion grows. Picnickers once started on their way come
scurrying back for forgotten bundles.* SCIPIO *runs in at gate
in high excitement.*]

SCIPIO: [*Breathless; to* SERENA]: Ma, uh hab good news fuh
you!
SERENA: Wuh dat iz?

SCIPIO: De ban'mastuh suh uh kin be uh offun!

[*The song breaks out in greater volume.*]
"Ent it haa'd tuh be uh nigguh!
Ent it haa'd tuh be uh nigguh!
Ent it haa'd tuh be uh nigguh!
'Kase you cyan' git you right w'en you do.
Uh binnuh sleep 'puntop uh pile uh lumbuh
Jis' ez happy ez Uh kin be,
When uh w'ite man wake me f'um me slumbuh
Suh, 'You hab tuh wu'k now 'kase you free.'"

[*Other voices are calling back and forth:* "Dem leetle nigguh kin sho' play!" "Ent you ready?" "Time fuh gone Kittywah!" *The band plays with more abandon.* BESS *wears the expression of a dreamer who sees herself in the midst of the merrymakers. Her feet begin to shuffle in time to the music.* PORGY *does not look up, but his eyes watch the shuffling feet.*]

PORGY: [*Mournfully*]: Bess, you cyan' tell me you ent wan' fuh go!

[*The Negroes troop across the court all carrying their baskets. In twos and threes they go out at the gate. Among the last to go,* MARIA *comes hurrying from her shop carrying a gigantic basket. Turns to follow the others. Sees* PORGY *and* BESS. *Hesitates. As though afraid of being left behind, turns again toward gate. Then resolutely sets down her basket.*]

MARIA: Wuh wrong wid you, Sistuh? Ent you know you gwi' be late fuh de picnic?

[*A sudden wave of happiness breaks over* BESS'S *face. She is too surprised to answer.*]

PORGY: Bess say 'e yent figguh fuh go!

MARIA: [*Crosses rapidly to them*]: 'Co'se 'e gwine! Eb'rybody gwine. 'E haffuh he'p me wid me baskut. Weh you hat?

[*Reaches hat just inside door and puts it on* BESS'S *head.*]

PORGY: [*Taking sash from pocket and holding it out to*
BESS]: Yuh me sash, Bess.

[MARIA *unties* BESS'S *apron. Throws it through door. Takes sash
from* PORGY, *pins is across* BESS'S *breast, jerking her peremp-
torily about to save time. Then starts for her basket.*]

MARIA: Come 'long, now!

BESS: [*Hesitating*]: Uh sho' ent wan' lef' you, Porgy.

PORGY: [*Happily*]: Uh too happy you gwine!

MARIA: Ent you gwi' he'p me wid dis baskut? [BESS *hurries to
her and takes one handle of basket.*] See you attuhw'ile,
Porgy. [MARIA *crosses rapidly to gate. To keep her hold on the
basket,* BESS *is forced to hurry.*]

BESS: [*Looking back*]: 'Bye, Porgy!

[MARIA *apparently seeing the others far ahead and anxious not to
be left behind, breaks into a lumbering run, dragging* BESS
after her. BESS *is waving to* PORGY *as she goes.*

*The voices of the Negroes grow fainter. Then the last distant
crashes of the band are heard, and the court is quiet.*

PORGY *sits on his doorstep dreaming, gazing happily into space,
rocking a little. Takes pipe from his pocket, knocks out ashes;
lights it.*

*Across the sunlit walls falls the shadow of the buzzard flying
lazily over the court.* PORGY *remains in happy abstraction,
oblivious of the bird. Puffs leisurely at his pipe.*

*The shadow hovers over his door; then falls across his face. He
looks up suddenly and sees the bird. Swift terror sweeps into
his face.*]

PORGY: [*Frantically*]: Git 'way f'um yuh! Don' you light! Git

'way f'um yuh, you yeddy me? Git 'way! [*He waves futile
arms at it. The bird continues to hover over him.*] Git out!
Somebody fetch de broom! Don' light obuh me do', you
debble. He'p! Somebody he'p me! Oh Gawd! [*He struggles
down the steps and at last reaches the brick.*

The shadow wings of the bird close as it comes to rest directly over
PORGY'S *door. Grasping the brick, he again looks up to take
aim. His fingers slowly relax, and the brick falls to the
ground.*] Ent no use, now. Ent no use. 'E done light.
[PORGY *regains his seat on step and sits looking up at the
bird with an expression of hopelessness as the curtain falls.*]

CURTAIN

Scene Two

*Kittiwah Island. Moonlight revealiang a narrow strip of
sand backed by a tangled palmetto thicket. In the distance (right)
the band is playing "Ent It Haa'd Tuh Be Uh Nigguh."*

JAKE, MINGO, *and several others troop across stage from left
to right, swinging apparently empty baskets.*

MINGO: Dis bin some picnic. Lawd, Uh ti'ed!

JAKE: [*Swinging his basket in a circle*]: Dis baskut mo' lightuh
fuh fetch back den fuh tote obuh yuh! [*Breaks into
song: "Ent It Haa'd" etc. The others join in. They go off
right, their song growing fainter in distance.*

SERENA *and* LILY *enter, followed a moment later by* BESS *and*
MARIA. MARIA *is puffing, out of breath.*]

MARIA: Uh yent no han' fuh walk fas' wid me belly fill! [*Stops
abruptly. Looks about her on ground.*]

SERENA: Sistuh, ef you ent mek'ace, you gwi' miss de boat!

MARIA: 'E bin right 'bout yuh weh Uh loss me pipe. Uh 'membuh de palmettuh bin sawtuh twis'up luk dat.

LILY: Mek you loss you pipe?

MARIA: [*Searching ground. The others help her*]: Uh binnuh set 'neet' de tree duh smoke, en' Uh see uh plat-eye duh look 'puntop me t'ru de palmettuh leabe. 'Fo' you kin crack you teet', Uh gone f'um yuh, 'cep' me pipe ent gone wid me!

LILY: How de plat-eye stan'?

MARIA: Two big fiah-ball eye duh watch me!

SERENA [*Scornfully*]: Plat-eye! You read ennyt'ing een de Bible 'bout plat-eye?

MARIA: Uh ent haffuh read 'bout'um! Uh shum duh look 'puntop me t'ru de palmettuh leabe!

SERENA: Jis' lukkuh you hab buzzut seddown 'puntop you table day 'fo' yistiddy, en' you study you head fuh fin' bad luck fuh blame on'um.

MARIA: Bad luck! Ent Uh done loss me pipe wuh Uh binnuh smoke fuh twenty yeah, en' me Ma done smoke 'fo' me?

LILY: Uh ent nebbuh lub fuh sleep wid no rattlesnake! Leh we go 'fo' de boat lef'!

MARIA: Ef dat boat gone bidout me, dey gwi' be some sick nigguh tuh Catfish Row w'en Uh git back! [*Steamboat whistles off right.* MARIA *answers it.*] Hol' on, Uh yent gwine 'tell Uh fin' me pipe!

BESS: Maria, you bes' gone 'long, en' leh we look fuh'rum. Us kin walk mo' fas'tuh den you.

MARIA: [*Pointing left*]: Mebbe Uh loss'um uh leetle fudduh dat way. [BESS *begins to search at left and wanders off left, her eyes combing the ground.*] En' mebbe 'e bin uh leetle fudduh dat way! [*Goes off right searching.* LILY *follows.* SERENA *continues her search on stage.*]

LILY: [*Off right*]: Uh yent shum no'weh! Come, leh we go!

MARIA: [*Farther in distance*]: Uh gwi' fin'um!

[*From the blackness of the thicket two eyes can be seen watching* SERENA. *As she turns in her quest, she sees them. For a moment, she is motionless; then her breath catches in a shuddering gasp of horror, and she flees swiftly off right. A snatch of the song rises suddenly in distance and quickly dies down again.* BESS *comes on from left, her head bent, still searching.*

A great black hand creeps slowly out among the palmetto branches and draws them aside. BESS *hears the sound. Straightens, stands rigid, listening.*]

BESS: [*In a low, breathless voice*]: Crown?

CROWN: You know berry well dis Crown! [*She turns and looks at him. He partly emerges from the thicket, naked to the waist, his cotton trousers frayed away to the knees.*] Uh see you lan', en' Uh binnuh wait all day fuh you. Uh mos' dead on dis dam' i'lun'!

BESS: [*Looks at him slowly*]: You ent look mos' dead. You mo'bigguh den ebbuh!

CROWN: Uh hab 'nuf bittle! Bu'd aig, oshtuh en' t'ing. Uh mos' dead wid de lonesome. Nobody fuh gib' de time ub day. Lawd Uh glad you come!

BESS: Uh cyan' stay, Crown. De boat gwi' lef'me!

CROWN: You hab some happy dus' wid you?

BESS: No!

CROWN: Come on! Ent you hab uh leetle tetch?

BESS: No! Uh yent! Uh done t'ru wid dope!

[CROWN *laughs loudly.*]

CROWN: 'E sho' do uh lonesome man good fuh 'e 'ooman come fuh mek joke wid'um.

BESS: Uh yent mek joke. En' Uh hab sump'n mo' fuh tell you, fuh true!

CROWN: Fus' you bes' liss'n yuh wuh Uh hab fuh tell you. Uh gwi' wait yuh ontel cott'n come een, den de lib'n' easy. Daby gwi' hide you en' me een de Sabunnuh boat. Who you duh lib wid now?

BESS: Uh libb'n' wid Porgy!

CROWN: [*Laughing*]: You sho' hab funny tas'e fuh mens, but dat you bidness. Uh yent min' who you tek-up wid w'en Uh yent dey. 'Cep' 'membuh wuh Uh tell you! Attuh 'bout two week, Uh gwi' come git you.

BESS: [*With an effort*]: Crown, Uh hab sump'n' fuh tell you.

CROWN: Well, wuh 'e yiz?

BESS: Uh sawtuh change me way.

CROWN: Wuh way dat you sawtuh change?

BESS: Sence Uh binnuh lib wid Porgy, Uh duh lib deestunt.

CROWN: You yeddy wuh Uh tell you, enty? W'en de two week done gone Uh gwi' come fuh you, en' you gwine. Onless you wan' meet you Gawd! You onduhstan'?

BESS: Crown, Uh tell you Uh done change. Uh gwi' stay wid Porgy fuh good. [*He seizes her by the arm and draws her savagely toward him. The steamboat whistles.*] Tu'n me loose! Uh gwi' miss de boat!

CROWN: Anudduh boat gwine day attuh tuhmorruh!

BESS: Swaytogawd, Uh tell you de trute! Porgy me man now!

CROWN: [*Jeering at her*]: Uh yent hab uh laugh sence two, t'ree week!

BESS: Tek you hot han' off me! Uh tell you Uh gwi' stay wid Porgy fuhr'ebbuh!

CROWN: You cyan' tell me you rudduh lib wid dat crawl'n' cripple den wid Crown!

BESS: [*Taking a propitiatory tone*]: 'E fuh true, Crown. Uh de onlies' 'ooman Porgy ebbuh hab. Ef all de odduh nigguh gone back tuh Catfish Row tonight, en' Uh yent gone home tuh Porgy, 'e gwi' stan' same lukkuh leetle chile wuh loss 'e Ma! [CROWN, *still holding her, throws back his head and laughs.* BESS *begins to be frightened.*] You kin laugh, but Uh tell you Uh change!

CROWN: You change, fuh true! You ent nebbuh bin dis much fun!

[*The boat whistles. She tries to pull away. He stops laughing and holds her tighter with lowering look. Draws her nearer.*]

BESS: Lemme go, Crown! You kin git plenty odduh 'ooman!

CROWN: Wuh Uh wan' wid odduh 'ooman? Uh hab 'ooman! Dat 'ooman duh you!

BESS: [*Trying flattery*]: You know how 'e alltime stan' wid you, Crown. You ent nebbuh lack 'ooman. Lookuh you ches', en' lookuh dem aa'm. Dey 'nuf gal wuh look mo'bettuh den me! You know how 'e alltime bin wid you en' me. De fibe yeah Uh bin you 'ooman, you kick me een de skreet, den w'en you ready fuh me 'gen, you w'issle, en' Uh right dey duh lick you han'. Bess ole 'ooman now! Wuh you wan' wid'um? [*She sees that her flattery has failed and is terrified.*] De boat gwi' lef' me! Lemme go, Crown! Uh gwi' come back fuh see yuh! Swaytogawd. Uh gwi' come 'long de Friday boat! Jis' lemme go now! Uh cyan' stay out yuh all night! Uh too 'f'aid. T'ing duh moobe 'bout een de t'ickit! Rattlesnake en't'ing! Lemme go, Crown! Tek you han' off me!

CROWN: [*Holding her and looking steadily at her*]: No man ebbuh tek 'ooman 'way f'um Crown. 'E gwi' be big joke on'um ef 'e loss 'e 'ooman tuh uh man wuh ent hab [*Draws her closer*] no laig needuh gizzut. So you change? [*Grips her more tightly. Looks straight into her eyes.*] Wuh you suh tuh dat?

BESS: [*Summoning the last of her resolution*]: Uh suh Uh gwi' stay wid Porgy!

[*His jaw shoots forward, and his huge shoulder muscles bulge and set. Slowly his giant hands close around her throat. He brings his eyes still closer to hers. The boat whistles long and loud, but neither gives sign of hearing it. After a moment,* CROWN *laughs with satisfaction at what he sees in* BESS'S *eyes.*

His hands leave her throat and clasp her savagely by the shoulders. BESS *throws back her head with a wild hysterical laugh.*]

CROWN: Uh know you ent change! 'E alltime gwi' be de same wid you en' me! You yeddy? [*He swings her about and hurls her face forward through an opening in the thicket. Then, with a low laugh, he follows her. She regains her balance and goes on ahead of him. The band is still playing, but growing faint in the distance.*]

CURTAIN

ACT THREE

ACT THREE

Scene One

*St. Michael's chimes the half hour. Curtain. The court before
dawn. Lights in a few windows:* MARIA'S, JAKE'S, PORGY'S.
The fishermen are preparing for an early departure.

JAKE: [*Coming from his door*]: Us ent hab no mo' time! [*Calls
to men in* MARIA'S *shop]:* Come on mens! 'E mos' dayclean!
Leh'we'go!

[CLARA *comes from their room, the baby in her arms. Her eyes
are anxious and reproachful, but she says nothing.*]

JIM: [*Coming from* MARIA'S *shop, wiping his mouth*]: You ready,
Jake? Time fuh gone!

JAKE: Come'leh'we'go!
[MARIA *appears in her doorway, wiping hands on her apron.*]

MARIA: Uh hope you hab good luck, Jake.

[JAKE *quickly takes baby from* CLARA'S *arms, kisses it hurriedly,
and returns it to* CLARA.]

JAKE: 'Bye, Big Boy!

[BESS'S *voice is heard from her room, droning in delirium. All
the Negroes stop suddenly to listen.*]

BESS: Aight'een mile tuh Kittywah---aight'een mile---
palmettuh bresh 'long de sho'---rattlesnake en' t'ing!

[JAKE *crosses to* PORGY'S *window.*]

JAKE: How Bess iz dis mawnin'?
[PORGY *appears at window.*]

PORGY: 'E yent no bettuh!

JAKE: 'E head tek'way?
[PORGY *nods.*]

BESS: Bess gwi' fin' you pipe, Maria! Bess gwi' fin'um fuh yuh!

[JAKE *shakes his head sadly. Hurriedly recrosses to the other men. They go toward gate together,* CLARA *following.*]

JIM: Uh bet de ketch us mek yistiddy no'bigguh den enny wuh ebbuh mek 'roun' yuh!

NELSON: Us bes' mek de mo'res' ub dis day. De cloud stan' lukkuh 'e gwi' wedduh!

JAKE: Ent you know you ent fuh talk so 'fo' me 'ooman? You ent yeddy'um duh aa'gyfy eb'ry day?

[*Laughs.*] Shum? 'E ent crack 'e teet'. Uh done lead' um tuh me han'. 'Bye, Clara.
[JAKE *gives* CLARA *a hurried, affectionate pat and follows the other men as they troop out the gate, talking and laughing. The gate clangs shut behind them.* CLARA *goes silently into her room, closes door.*]

BESS: 'E mus'e right yuh 'puntop de groun'. Bess gwi' fin'um!
[BESS'S *voice drones on.*]

[MARIA, *in her doorway, listens a moment. Then crosses to* POR-GY'S *door; hesitates, awed by the mystery of delirium.* SERENA *silently crosses the court and joins* MARIA. *They listen a moment longer.*]

SERENA: [*In a low voice*]: 'E stillyet out 'e head?
[MARIA *nods. They stand silent.*]

BESS: [*From the room*]: Aight'een mile tuh Kittywah--- palmettuh bresh by de sho'. Aight'een mile tuh Kittywah.

[PETER *appears outside the gate. He seems older and feebler, but his face is joyful. Pushes gate open, comes into court, looking eagerly about. Sees the two women and crosses toward them.*]

PETER: How eb'rybody iz?

[*They turn and see him.*]

MARIA: [*Joyfully*]: T'engk Gawd, Petuh duh home!

SERENA: Come'yuh, Lilly! Daddy Petuh come home! Lawd, us glad fuh see yuh!

[LILY *comes running from her door. Hurries to* PETER *and greets him joyfully.*]

LILY: Do, Jedus, yuh me ole gran'daddy!

PETER: Uh mos' t'ink Uh yent gwi' nebbuh see Catfish Row 'gen!

[BESS'S *voice rises in a sudden wail. The women turn awe-stricken faces toward* PORGY'S *door.* PETER, *who has not heard, is mystified by their expressions. His words die away. He looks questioningly from one to another.* BESS *again takes up her monotonous refrain.*]

BESS: Palmettuh bresh sawtuh twis'up-------rattlesnake en't'ing.

PETER: Wuh ail Bess?

MARIA: [*Shouting into his ear*]: Porgy 'ooman berry sick!

LILY: [*Shouting*]: 'E ractify een 'e min'!

PETER: How long 'e stan' so?

MARIA: Mo'nuh week! Ebbuh sence us hab picnic tuh Kitty-wah.

SERENA: 'E gone off tuh 'ese'f en' git loss een de palmettuh t'ickit. De boat lef', en' Bess ent git home fuh de two day!

BESS: N'min, Maria, Uh gwi' fin' you pipe.....aight'een mile tuh Kittyway...aight'een mile...

PORGY: [*Within room, soothingly*]: You awright, Bess. You yuh wid Porgy now.

BESS: [*Monotonously*]: Palmettuh bresh by de sho'.

[MARIA, SERENA, *and* PETER *stand wide-eyed, looking in at the door. They do not go too near.*]

PORGY: You yuh wid Porgy en' nutt'n' cyan' hu't you. Cool wedduh gwi' come soon en' cyo' you febuh.

PETER: [*Shaking his head*]: Dat 'ooman berry sick, fuh true! [*The women nod.*]

PORGY: You 'membuh w'en de cool win' come en' fetch de smell ub pine tree? En' how de staar all shine lukkuh de buckruh silbuh? Den eb'rybody git well. You jis' watch wuh Porgy say.

[*Silence in the room.* CLARA *comes from her door carrying her baby, crosses to the gate and stands looking out toward the sea. After a moment,* PORGY *comes from his door, softly closes it behind him.*]

PORGY: Mebbe 'e gwi' sleep now. [*Sinks wearily on step.*]
[*Dully*]: Glad fuh see you, Petuh. Bess bin sick fuh uh week. Uh yent know wuffuh do!
[*A moment of silence.*]

PETER: Uh know wuffuh do! Sen'um tuh de hawsspittle. [*Blank consternation.* MARIA *is first to find her voice.*]

MARIA: [*Speaking into his ears*]: Fuh Gawd sake, Petuh, ent you know dey let nigguh die tuh de hawsspittle, so dey kin gib'um tuh de stoodun'?

PETER: Dey ent gib'um tuh de stoodun' 'tell dem done fuh dead. Den dey cyan' hu't'um none. En' Uh know, fuh true, dey uh w'ite nuss tuh de hawsspittkle wuh uh pyo' ainjul wid sick nigguh. Ef Uh tek sick tuhmorruh Uh gwi' tuhr'um, en' Uh gwi' do wuhebbuh 'e say. Uh wan' tek

cyah me cawcuss w'ile Uh libb'n'. Uh yent cyah 'bout'um
w'en Uh done fuh dead.

LILY: [*Shouting*]: You ent cyah ef you git cut'up en' scattuh
'bout, 'stidduh bury deestunt een Gawd own grabeyaa'd?

PETER: Uh yent mean Uh yent cyah, fuh true, but Uh t'ink
Gawd gwi' onduhstan' de sukkumstan', en' mek 'lowance.

PORGY: [*Moaning*]: Oh, Gawd! Don' leh'um tek me Bess tuh
de hawsspittle!

SERENA: [*In injured tone*]: You mus'e fuhgit Uh done pray Clara
baby out dat cunwulshun, enty? Dey ent nebbuh bin uh sick
pussun, needuhso cawpse een Catfish Row wuh Uh yent
pray fuh. Uh duh pray fuh de sinnuh en' de right'ous,
alltwo!

PORGY: Fuh true, Sistuh, you pray fuhr'um! Dat sho' cyan'
hu't'um none.
[SERENA *closes her eyes and begins to sway.*]

SERENA: Oh, Jedus you done cyaam de watuh tuh de Sea ub
Gallyree!

PORGY: Amen!

SERENA: En' you done cas' de debble out de 'flicted time en'
time 'gen!

PETER: *Begins to sway.*] Oh, Jedus!

SERENA: Mek you ent lay you han' 'puntop we sistuh head?

LILY: Oh, me Farruh!

SERENA: En' sen' de debble out'um, down deep een de sea,
samelukkuh you duh do, time en' time 'gen!

PORGY: Time en' time 'gen!

SERENA: En' lif' dis po' cripple up out de dus'.

PETER: Hallylooyuh!

SERENA: En' lif'up 'e 'ooman, en' mek'um well, time en' time 'gen!

[*They sway a moment in silence. Then* SERENA *silently rises and departs. After a moment,* PETER *and* LILY *follow her.*]

MARIA: [*In a low voice*]: Haa'kee tuh me! You wan' Bess cyo', enty?

PORGY: 'Co'se Uh wan'um cyo'!

MARIA: Berrywellden! Mek you ent gone tuh Lody?

PORGY: Fuh mek cunjuh?

MARIA: You hab two dolluh, enty?

[PORGY *nods.*]

Den mek'ace en' gone tuh Lody! G'em de two dolluh en' ax'um fuh mek cunjuh fuh cas' de debble out'uh Bess!

[MINGO *has sauntered in and taken a seat at the table by* MARIA'S *door.*]

PORGY: 'Cep'n' Uh cyan' lef' Bess!

MINGO: Mawn'n', Maria! How 'bout some brekwus'?

MARIA: Come'yuh, Mingo!

[*He crosses to them.*]

Ef you do leetle job fuh Porgy, Uh gwi' gib' you free brekwus' w'en you git back. You know Lody, de cunjuh 'ooman, enty?

MINGO: 'Co'se! Eb'rybody know Lody.

MARIA: Mek'ace tuh Lody en' tell'um mus' wek cunjuh fuh cas' de debble out Bess. Porgy gwi' gib' you two dolluh fuh g'em!

[PORGY *has taken out his money bag and is counting out pennies.*]

MINGO: 'E uh long way tuh Lody house 'fo' brekwus'.

MARIA: Yeddy de nigguh! Ef you ent bin dead on you foot, you kin git dey en' back 'fo' de brekwus' done cook.

MINGO: Wuh you hab fuh brekwus'?

MARIA: Uh hab butt meat fuh greese you mout', en' cawnbread en' muhlassis fuh tas'e you mout'.

MINGO: How 'bout some shaa'k steak?

MARIA: Liss'n nigguh! Uh ent saa'b no free brekwus' alley cat.

MINGO: [Belligerently]: Whodat you duh call alley cat?

MARIA: [Despairingly]: Dis nigguh ent know nutt'n'! Ent you ebbuh bin tuh stylish res'runt wuh hab de bittle name write 'puntop de wall, en' you kin chuse wuh you wan' nyam? Dat alley caa't; een dis res'runt Uh recide wuh you gwi' nyam! Uh yent saa'b alley cat!

PORGY: Uh gwi' pay you twenty-fibe cent fuh gone tuh Lody.

MINGO: Berrywellden! Twenty-fibe cent mek'um mo'closuh!

PORGY: [Handing him money]: Yuh de two dolluh fuh Lody, en' de twenty-fibe cent fuh you'se'f.
[MINGO starts for gate.]

MARIA: Uh gwi' pit de brekwus' 'pun de table tuhreckly. Mek'ace, 'fo' 'e git col'!

MINGO: Uh gwi' git back 'fo' you kin crack you teet'!
[Goes out gate and off to left. St. Michael's chimes the three-quarter hour.]

MARIA: 'E mos' fibe by de clock! Mingo cyan' tek dat long tuh git tuh Lody. W'en fibe o'clock come, Lody gwi' hab de cunjuh done mek.

PORGY: [Eagerly]: You t'ink cunjuh gwi' cyo'um?

MARIA: Uh yent t'ink! Uh know! Watch wuh Uh say, me brudduh. W'en fibe o'clock come, Bess gwi' cyo'.

[*Crosses to her shop. Goes about her work.*]
[SERENA *has gone to work at her tubs. She now calls to* CLARA, *who still stands gazing out through gate.*]

SERENA: Wuh you duh look fuh, Clara? De boat mus'e clean gone by dis time!

CLARA: De boat done bin gone!

MARIA: [*Working at her table*]: You ent hab no cause fuh worry 'bout you man. Dis gwi' be uh good day!

CLARA: De watuh ent nebbuh stan' so daa'k!

MARIA: You ebbuh shum stan' so cyaam?

CLARA: No, 'e too cyaam, en' me Bline Gawd tell me mus' liss'n fuh harricane bell! [*Crosses to* SERENA. *Sits on bench.*] Leh me seddown yuh, en' you onrabble you mout'.

MARIA: [*Who has crossed to pump with kettle*]: Uh hab uh feel'n'.

SERENA: Wuh you duh talk 'bout?

MARIA: Uh hab uh feel'n', w'en Bess bin loss tuh Kittywah, 'e yent bin loss, fuh true, 'e bin wid Crown!

SERENA: [*Her face darkening*]: You hab uh feel'n' dat nigguh dey tuh Kittywah?

MARIA: Uh figguh 'e dey een de palmettuh t'ickit. En' w'en Uh yeddy wuh Bess suh w'en 'e out 'e head, Uh sho' Crown tuh Kittywah, en' Bess bin dey wid' um.

CLARA: You b'leebe Bess still run wid dat nigguh?

MARIA: Dat sawtuh man ent haffuh worry 'e head 'bout fin' 'ooman!

SERENA: Bess gwi' stay wid Porgy, ef 'e know wuh good fuhr'um.

MARIA: 'E know, awright! En' 'e lub Porgy, but ef dat nigguh
come attuhr'um, 'e gwine! Dey ent gwi' be nobody lef' wid
Porgy but de goat.

[*As* MARIA *speaks,* PORGY *comes from his door. The other women
sign to* MARIA *to be careful. Seeing* PORGY, *she drops the subject and returns to her shop.*]

SERENA: [*Piling clothes in basket*]: Come 'long Clara. He'p me
wid dese clo'es!

[CLARA, *holding baby on one arm, takes one handle of basket.*
SERENA *lifts the other. They carry it through* SERENA'S *door.*
PORGY *sits on his doorstep, his face tense, waiting.*
DADDY PETER *comes from his door followed by* LILY, *who carries
the honey tray. She places it on his head and returns to room,
closing the door.* PETER *crosses toward gate, beginning
instantly to chant.*]

PETER: Uh hab honey---You hab honey?---Yaas mam, Uh hab
honey?---You hab honey cheap?

[*A woman leans from an upper window and calls.*]

THE WOMAN: Oh, Honey man! Honey man!

PETER: [*Going on*] Yaas mam, me honey cheap!

THE WOMAN: Hol'up! Uh wan' some honey!
[PETER *goes out gate and off to right.*]

PETER: You hab honey een de comb?---Yaas mam, Uh hab
honey een de comb.---Yuh come de honey man!---Uh hab
honey!
[PORGY *sits waiting. St. Michael's begins to chime the hour.*
PORGY *grows suddenly rigid.*
As the chimes continue, MARIA *comes to her door way and stands
motionless, also listening. She and* PORGY *gaze at each other
across court with tense, expectant faces. The chimes cease.*]

PORGY: [*In low, vibrant voice*]: Oh, Gawd! Dis de time!

[*St. Michael's strikes five. As* PORGY *and* MARIA *still wait
motionless,* BESS'S *voice is heard, weakly.*]

BESS: Porgy?
[PORGY *and* MARIA *are both electrified by the sound. They gaze at
each other with joyful faces, but for a second neither moves.*]
Porgy, dat duh you, enty? Mek you en't talk tuh me?

PORGY: [*With a half-laugh that breaks in a sob*]: T'engk Gawd!
T'engk Gawd!
[BESS *appears in the doorway in her white nightgown. She is very
weak.*]

BESS: Uh lonesome yuh all by me'se'f.
[MARIA *crosses to her quickly. Gently assists her as she lowers
herself to seat beside* PORGY.]

BESS: 'E hot een de room. Uh kin set yuh een de cool?

MARIA: Uh gwi' git you blankut.

PORGY: Bess need fuh gone back tuh bed, enty?

MARIA: [*Going past them into room*]: Lem'lone! Ent Uh tell you
dat cunjuh gwi' cyo'um?

BESS: Uh bin sick, enty?

PORGY: Oh, Bess! Bess!

BESS: Wuh wrong?
[*Almost sobbing with relief*]: You bin berry sick! T'engk Gawd
de cunjuh cyo' you!
[MARIA *reappears with blanket, which she wraps about* BESS.]

MARIA: Bess, you cyan' set yuh berry long. [*Returns to her
shop.*]

PORGY: Uh hab you back, Bess!

BESS: How long Uh bin sick?

PORGY: Fuh uh week! W'en you come back f'um Kittywah you eye bin samelukkuh fiah-ball, en' Maria git you een de bed, en' you ent know me.
[BESS *suddenly catches her breath in a stifled sob.*]

Wuh wrong, Bess?

BESS: Ef me head ent bin tek'way wid de febuh, Uh s'pose Uh yent binnuh come back!

PORGY: You ent mean fuh come back tuh Porgy?
[*She begins to moan hysterically.*]

BESS: No! Uh mean 'e wrong fuh Uh come back!

PORGY: [*Soothingly*]: Bess, you ent haffuh fret! Uh know you bin wid Crown!
[BESS *draws in her breath sharply, then speaks in a whisper.*]

BESS: Porgy, how you know dat?

PORGY: You binnuh talk 'bout'um w'en you out you head.

BESS: Wuh uh suh!

PORGY: You duh talk tangledy, but Gawd gib' cripple onduhstan' fuh know t'ing strong mens ent fuh know!

BESS: Porgy, you wan' me fuh gone, enty?

PORGY: [*Looks at her keenly.*] No, Uh yent wan' you fuh go.
[*A moment of silence.*]

You ent nebbuh lie tuh me, Bess!

BESS: Uh yent nebbuh lie tuh you, Porgy!
[*Another silence.*]

PORGY: How 'e stan' 'tween you en' Crown?

BESS: [*After a pause*]: 'E gwi' come fuh me w'en cott'n come een town.

PORGY: You gwine?

BESS: Uh tell'um Uh gwine!

[PORGY *turns his head from her and sits looking straight before him. After a moment,* BESS *reaches out timidly and lays her hand on his arm. Then she tries to encircle it with her fingers.*]

Gawd, Porgy! You hab aa'm samelukkuh steebuhdo'! Mek you muskle pull up luk dat?

[*He looks at her, his face set and stern. She cowers, her hand still on his arm.*]

'E mek me 'f'aid!

[*A pause.*]

PORGY: You ent haffuh 'f'aid. Uh yent nebbuh try tuh keep no 'ooman wuh ent wan' stay. Ef you wan' gone wid Crown, dat you bidness!

BESS: Uh yent wan' gone, Porgy!

[PORGY *looks at her with hope.*]

BESS: But Uh yent you kin'. W'en Crown pit 'e han' on me, Uh run tuhr'um luk watuh. Someday 'gen 'e gwi' pit 'e han' on me t'roat, en' 'e gwi' be same luk Uh duh die. Uh haffuh tell you de trute. W'en dat time come, Uh gwi' go!

[*Silence.*]

PORGY: [*In a whisper*]: Bess, ef dey ent bin no Crown. Ef 'e bin jis' me en' you. Wuh den?

[*She looks into his face with an expression of yearning. Then, suddenly, the weakness of her illness sweeps down upon her and she breaks out hysterically, trembling with fear.*]

BESS: Fuh Gawd sake, Porgy! Don' leh dat man come en' handl' me! Ef you wan' me, lemme stay!

[*Her voice rises hysterically, broken by sobs.*]

Ef 'e jis' ent pit 'e hot han' on me, Uh kin 'membuh Uh happy, en' be good! [*The sobs overcome her.*]

PORGY: Dey, now, Bess.
[*Pats her arm soothingly, waiting for the storm to spend itself. She
grows suddenly quiet, except for occasional silent, rending
sighs.*]
You ent haffuh 'f'aid! You hab you man, enty? You hab Porgy fuh
tek cyah ub you. Wuh kind'uh nigguh you t'ink you hab fuh
leh anudduh nigguh tek 'ooman? No, suh? You hab you
man! You hab Porgy!

[BESS *has become quiet. A pause.*]
Come 'long. You done set yuh too long. Porgy gwi' he'p you
back tuh bed.
[*He draws himself up by the door frame.* BESS *rises unsteadily
and, with a hand on his arm, they make their way into the
room.* PORGY *closes the door behind them.*

MINGO *appears outside the gate, steadies himself against it, then
staggers through and crosses to* MARIA'S *table. Slumps into
chair. Pounds on table, then buries head in his hands.* MARIA
comes to doorway.]

MARIA: Dat you, Mingo? Gawd A'mighty, how you git drunk so
fas'? [*Goes into shop and immediately returns with breakfast
things on a tray. Begins putting them before him.*] Uh bet
you drink dat rot gut skrate! Ent you know you mus'
puhlute w'isk'y wid watuh?

MINGO: [*Pushing dishes away*]: Uh yent wan' dat stuff! Uh wan'
shaa'k steak!

MARIA: [*Hands on hips*]: You wan' shaa'k steak! You t'ink Uh
gwi' gib' shaa'k steak wid free brekwus'?

MINGO: Uh tell you Uh wan' shaa'k steak! [*With uncertain
movements, draws a handful of change from pocket.*]

MARIA: [*Mollified*]: 'Co'se, ef you gwi' pay fuhr'um!
[MINGO *spills the money in a pile on table. It is all pennies.*
MARIA *stares at it, then at him. Her eyes are suddenly filled
with suspicion.*]

Weh you git dat money f'um?
[MINGO *looks up at her stupidly. She speaks in a ferocious whisper.*]

Weh you git dem penny?
[MINGO *seems to try to recollect.*]

'E all penny, samelukkuh Porgy git w'en 'e baig!
[*She suddenly seizes him, jerks him to his fee.*] Dat Porgy money wuh 'e gib' you fuh Lody!
[MINGO *opens his mouth to protest, searching wildly for words.*]

MARIA: Don' lie tuh me, nigguh!

MINGO: Uh jis' tek 'nuf fuh uh leetle drink!
[MARIA *gives him a savage shake which seems to spill out further words.*]
Uh t'ink Lody done moobe. Uh cyan' fin'um! [*With weak bravado*]: Lemme go ole lady! [*Tries to shake off her grip.*]
[MARIA *holds him tighter and brings her face close to his. His eyes suddenly meet hers, and he sees a look of such cold ferocity that he quails and sobs with terror.*]

MINGO: Oh, Jedus!

MARIA: You low down houn'! You drink-up uh po' dy'n' 'ooman cunjuh money, en' ent lef'um nutt'n' but fuh us pray obuhr'um. Liss'n tuh me, nigguh.
[*Slowly and impressively*]: Fuh you own good, Uh gwi' lock you up een me house ontell you sobuh 'nuf tuh keep you mout' shet. Den mebbe Uh gwi' loose you. But Uh yent gwi' nebbuh let you out me sight. Ef you ebbuh tell Porgy dat you ent 'li'buh dat mestidge tuh Lody, Uh gwi' hab nigguh blood on me han' w'en Uh stan' jedgemunt! You yeddy me, enty?

[MINGO, *unable to speak, nods. She swings him suddenly about, hurls him into her room, and closes the door on him. Wipes her face on apron, looks with mystified expression toward* PORGY'S *closed door. Baffled.*]

Jedus mus'e cyo' Bess, attuh all! [*Considers a moment. Takes a
few steps toward* PORGY'S *door. Then stops, with decision.*]
No! dam' ef 'E do'um! 'E yent hab it een'um! [*Goes into
her room. Bangs door behind her.*]
[*For a moment, the court is empty and and silent. Suddenly, the
silence is broken by the deep, ominous clang of a bell, very
different from the silver tone of St. Michael's.
Instantly, every resident of Catfish Row, excepting* MINGO *and*
BESS, *is in the court or leaning from his window. Having
come, they now stand motionless, scarcely breathing, listening to the Bell.*
CLARA, *with her baby, has come from* SERENA'S *door, her eyes
bright with terror.*]

MARIA: Mus'e de bell fuh de hot wabe! 'E yent gwi' ring
mo'nuh twelbe time.

LILY: [*Who has been counting half audibly*]: ten---'leben---
twelbe----
[*For a moment no one breathes. Then the bell rings on. Every
face is suddenly rigid with horror.*]

CLARA: [*Wildly*]: Twenty! [*She runs to the gate and looks off
left.*]

SERENA: [*Following and seeking to comfort her*]: Dat bell mus'e
wrong! You membuh de las' harricane? 'E tek two day fuh
git yuh, enty?

ANNIE: Eb'ryt'ing cyaam, now. No win' duh blo'!
[*All the Negroes have gone to the gate and are gazing off to left.*]

PORGY: [*From his window*]: How de Custum House flag stan'?

SERENA: 'E dey dey 'puntop'uh de pole!

MARIA: [*Seeing it too, relieved*]: You shum enty, Clara?

SERENA: [*Reassuringly to Clara*]: Uh shum! Dat ent no harricane flag!

MARIA: Eb'ryt'ing awright long ez de 'Merican flag wabe obuh de Custum House.
[*They are all gazing off left at the distant flag. Suddenly, a new wave of horror sweeps simultaneously over every face.* MARIA'S *speech breaks off with her lips still parted.*]

LILY: [*In a low, awed voice*]: Gawd! Dey done tek'um down!
[*They continue to gaze, fascinated, but* CLARA *turns away, back into the court. Her terror has given way to dull hopelessness.*]

CLARA: Uh yent need no harricane flag fuh tell me nutt'n'. No need fuh Uh liss'n fuhr'um now!

PORGY: W'en de mens see de flag, dey gwi' mek'ace en' come home.

CLARA: Dem awready tuh Blackfish Bank. Dey cyan' see de flag f'um dey.

ANNIE: [*Hysterically*]: How dem kin git back? Dey ent hab no win' fuh de sail.

MARIA: [*Sternly silencing her*]: Dey kin row een! De storm ent git yuh yet.

PORGY: Fuh true! 'E yent yuh yesong

LILY: Uh yent gwi' agguhnize 'bout t'ing wuh mos' likely ent gwi' happ'n.
[*There is a general babble of voices*]: Time 'nuf fuh worry w'en de storm come. Mebbe by tuhmorruh us gwi' hab some wedduh.
[*While they reassure themselves, the sea is darkening. The shutters of Catfish Row begin to flap back and forth in a sudden wind.* CLARA *stands watching the swinging shutters.*]

CURTAIN

Scene Two

*Before the rise of the curtain the sound of wind and water begins
and swiftly swells and rises. Through the wind the chimes
and bell of St. Michael's are heard, sometimes rising clear
and strong as the wind lulls, then lost completely in a sudden
gust.*
The curtain rises on SERENA'S *room, dim and shadowy in the
light of fluttering kerosene lamps. The Negroes are huddled
together in groups. A few have found seats on the chairs and
bed. Others sit on the floor. A small group at right, including*
SERENA *and* PETER, *are on their knees, swaying and singing.*
PORGY *and* BESS *sit together on the floor at left front.* CLARA
*stands motionless at window, her baby in her arms. Every
face is filled with fear. They shudder and draw closer together
as the wind rises.*

THE SINGERS: "Us gwi' all sing tuhgedduh dat day,
We gwi' all sing tuhgedduh dat day,
En' Uh gwi' fall 'pun me knee en' face de ris'n' sun,
Oh, Lawd hab mussy on me!"

MARIA: [*Speaking above the monotonous chant*]: Mek' you duh
stan' dey duh look, Clara? 'E too daa'k fuh you see ennyt-
'ing.

CLARA: [*Gazing out between slats of closed shutters; in a flat,
dull voice*]: Uh t'ink Uh see some light 'roun' de aige ub de
storm. 'E mus'e mos' dayclean.
[*In a sudden silence of the wind, a faint, distant sound is heard.*]

ANNIE: Wuh dat? Soun' lukkuh w'inny!

CLARA: Somebody po' hawss een de watuh!

PORGY: [*Moaning*]: Me po' leetle goat gwi' dead! Dat goat me
laig. Uh cyan' nebbuh walk 'gen!

MARIA: Dat goat berry smaa't, Porgy. 'E gwi' clim' 'pun de bed en' keep 'e head out de watuh. You watch!

PETER: You bes' come sing wid me, Clara. Dat mek you feel mo'bettuh.

CLARA: [*Suddenly hysterical*]: You sing'n' mos' ractify me min'. You binnuh sing de same sperritual sence dayclean yistiddy!

SERENA: [*Severely*]: Us wan' ready w'en de grabe gib'up de dead en' Gabrull blow' 'e hawn, enty?

SPORTING LIFE: Uh yent so sho' dis de Jedgemunt Day. Us hab wedduh 'fo' dis.

SERENA: 'Cep' 'e ent bin dis bad!

MINGO: Uh 'membuh Ma say w'en dem hab eart'quake, all de nigguh binnuh sing dat Jedgemunt Day sperrritual, en' wait fuh de soun' ub de hawn. 'E yent bin Jedgemunt Day den, en' 'e yent likely now.

SERENA: Dat mebbe so! 'Cep' dis ent no time fun tek chance.
[*Bursts again into song. Her group joins her.*]
[*The shutters suddenly fly apart and flap violently in the wind, drowning out the singing. The Negroes cower and draw closer together. Some of the men struggle to capture the flying shutters.* BESS *sits calm, gazing straight ahead of her.* PORGY *is watching her thoughtfully.*]

PORGY: [*In a brief moment of quiet*]: Bess, you ent 'f'aid?
[BESS *shakes her head. A pause.*] Mek you ent say nutt'n'?

BESS: Uh jis' binnuh t'ink!
[*The men finally lash the shutters together with rope.*]
You know wuh Uh dun t'ink 'bout, Porgy?

PORGY: You duh t'ink dis storm bad, fuh true, tuh Kittywah.
[BESS *nods.*]

BESS: Wabe lukkuh dis mus'e done wash clean 'cross de i'lun'.
[*After a moment, she lays her hand on his arm.* PORGY *looks
keenly into her eyes.*]

PORGY: You sorry, enty?

BESS: Uh sorry fuh enny man wuh lef' out een dis storm! But
Uh done stop liss'n fuh 'e step, now. Seem lukkuh you got
me fuh good, Porgy. [*Puts her hand in his.*]

PORGY: Uh done tell you dat how 'e stan'!
[*A distant roar is heard, coming steadily nearer.*]

LILY: [*Terror-stricken.*] Yuh 'e come!

SERENA: Oh, Mastuh, Uh ready!
[*The crash and roar sweep by.*]

MARIA: You kin shum, Clara?

CLARA: 'E somebody roof gwine by!

ANNIE: Gawd A'mighty!

PETER: Oh, Jedus hab mussy!

SERENA: Leh we sing!
[SERENA'S *group begins to sing, but before they have completed a
single line* CLARA *cries out loudly.*]

CLARA: Fuh Gawd sake sing sump'n' else!
[*The singers are startled into silence. A blank pause. Then* BESS
begins to sing, "Somebody Knock'n' tuh de Door"
[*And one by one the others join her till the whole room is singing.*]

ALL: Somebody knock'n' tuh de do'.
Somebody knock'n' tuh de do'.
Oh, Mary, oh, Maa'tha,
Somebody knock'n' tuh de do'.

'E duh moan, Lawd,
Somebody knock'n' tuh de do'.
'E duh moan, Lawd,
Somebody knock'n' tuh de do!
Oh, Mary, oh, Maa'tha,
Somebody knock'n' tuh de do'.

" 'E uh sinnuh, Lawd," etc.
" 'E me preechuh, Lawd," etc.
" 'E me Jedus, Lawd," etc.

[*The spiritual swells and gains in tempo; the rhythm of the patting and swaying grows. A few begin to shout.*]

PETER: Uh yeddy de't' knock'n' tuh de do'. [*Looks fearfully at
door.*]

[*His haunted expression draws the attention of the others. One by
one, they stop singing.*]

ANNIE: Wuh you suh, Daddy Petuh?
[*The singing stops, but the rhythm continues.*]

PETER: Uh yeddy de't' duh knock tuh de do'!
[*A horrified silence. All eyes turn to door.*]

LILY: [*In an awed whisper.*] 'E mus'e de't', eeduhso Petuh ent
able fuh yeddy'um.

MINGO: 'E yent yeddy nutt'n'! Nobody ent knock!

LILY: Yaas dey iz! Somebody dey dey.

PETER: De't' duh knock tuh de do'.

MARIA: Op'n de do'! Show'um dey ent nobody dey.

MINGO: Op'n'um yo'se'f!
[MARIA *rises and starts toward door.*]

LILY: [*Wildly*]: Uh tell you somebody dey, en' Petuh cyan'
yeddy no libb'n' pussun.

[MARIA *hesitates. A loud knock is heard. The Negroes immedi-*
ately burst into a pandemonium of terror. There are cries of
"Gawd hab mussy!" "Don' leh'um come een!'
The knock is repeated, louder. Some begin to pray, but the more
energetic begin piling furniture in front of door. "Bring dat
dressuh!" "Wedge'um 'neet' de knob," etc. *The door is*
shaken violently.]

BESS: Dey ent no use. Ef 'e de't', 'e gwi' come een ennyway!

MARIA: [*Now the most terrified of all*]: Oh, Gawd! Gawd! Don'
leh'um come een!

[*With a sucking sound of the wind, the door slowly opens, push-*
ing away the flimsy furniture. Shrieks of terror and prayers
fill the room.

CROWN, *bent double against the wind, enters. As one by one they*
gain courage to look toward the door, the prayers die away.
For a moment, the Negroes stare at him in silence. Then
there are cries of "Crown!" "Gawd, 'e Crown!"

BESS *sits silent, rigid.* PORGY *gazes at her searchingly.*]

CROWN: You uh fine bunch ub nigguh! Shut out you fr'en' een
dis wedduh!

SERENA: Who dat you fr'en'?

CROWN: Uh yiz you fr'en', Sistuh. Glad fuh see yuh! You still
duh greebe, or you hab anudduh man?

SERENA: Uh pray Gawd fuh hol'back me han'!

CROWN: [*Laughing*]: 'E gwi' hol'um, awright. You bes' try de
poleece.

MARIA: You know berrywell dat Serena mo' deestunt den tuh
gib' nigguh 'way tuh de poleece.

CROWN: [*To* SERENA]: 'Tween you Gawd en' you mannus, you
sho' mek t'ing saa'f fuh uh haa'd nigguh.
[*Sees* BESS.]

Dey de one Uh duh look fuh. Mek you ent come hail you man?

BESS: You ent me man!

CROWN: 'E sho' time fuh Uh git back. Dis ent no 'ooman uh man kin leabe. [*Looking at* PORGY]: You sho' ent done much fuh yo'se'f·w'ile Uh bin gone. Ent no man lef' 'cep' cripple?

BESS: [*Rising and facing him*]: Keep Progy out you mout'!

CROWN: Well, fuh Gawd sake! You jis' sorry fuhr'um, enty?

BESS: Uh done tell you Uh yent gwine wid you. Uh gwi' stay wid Porgy fuhr'ebbuh!

CROWN: Come'yuh, 'ooman! Ef you ent wan' meet you Gawd!

BESS: [*Holding her ground*]: Porgy me man, now!

CROWN: [*Laughing*]: You call dat uh man? Nebbuh min', Uh gwi' fuhgibe you en' tek you back.
[*Reaches for her.* BESS *violently repulses him.*]

BESS: Keep you han' off me!

SERENA: [*To* CROWN]: Ef you stay 'roun' yuh, somebody gwi' kill you, fuh sho'. Sence Uh bin Robbin wife, de buckruh gwi' figguh Uh do'um en' lock me up, so mebbe Uh do'um now, jis' dry 'long so!
[BESS *returns; to her seat by* PORGY.]

CROWN: [*Laughing*]: Mek you t'ink somebody gwi' kill me? Ef Gawd wan' me kill, 'e hab 'nuf chance 'tween yuh en' Kittywah. Us binnuh fight all de way f'um dat i'lan'. Fus' Gawd, den me! Dey ent nutt'n' Gawd lub mo'bettuh den scrap wid man. Gawd en' me fr'en'!

[*A terrific roar of wind.*]

SERENA: [*Terror-stricken*]: You fool! You ent hab mo' sense den tuh talk 'bout Gawd luk dat een dis storm? [*Another sudden gust.*]

CROWN: Yeddy dat? Gawd duh laugh!

PETER: 'E berry dainjus fuh we hab dat bad mout' nigguh 'mong we. Leh we sing tuh de Lawd!
[*A woman's voice leads the spiritual,* "Uh Hab tuh Meet de Jedgemunt."]

THE WOMEN: "All Uh know---

SEVERAL MEN: Un hab tuh meet de Jedgemunt.

THE WOMEN: "All Uh know---

THE MEN: Hab tuh meet de Jedgemunt.

THE WOMEN: "All Uh know---

THE MEN: Hab tuh meet de Jedgemunt.

TOGETHER: All Uh know, All Uh know, All Uh know---

THE WOMEN: "All Uh moan---

THE MEN: Uh hab tuh meet de Jedgemunt-----"
[*As the wind subsides, the spiritual rises strong and clear. The Negroes sing and sway for a moment uninterrupted.*]

CROWN: [*His voice rising above the singing*]: You mus' t'ink de Lawd berry easy fuh please, ef you t'ink 'e lub fuh yeddy dat!
[*They sing on.*] 'Ef 'e do'um samelukkuh 'e do me, you done g'em, de lonesome blues!

[*They continue to sing.* CROWN *shouts above singing.*]

CROWN: Quit dat! Uh yent come spang f'um Kittywah I'lan' fuh set-up wid no cawpse. Dem wuh cyan' wait fuh Jedgemunt Day, kin say goodbye en' step out de do'. Daddy Petuh, yuh you chance! De Jim Crow ready fuh gone en' you ent need no tickut!

[*Turning to* SERENA]: How 'about you, Sistuh? All aboa'd! Nobody ent ready fuh trabble?
[*A roar of wind.*]

CROWN: Dey go de strain! En' you miss you chance! [*The wind rises above the singing.* CROWN *shouts up at ceiling*]: Dat right! Drown'um out! Don' liss'n tuhr'um! Dey ent gib' you credik fuh no tas'e een sing'n'. How 'bout dis, Big Fr'en'? [*Sings*]:
"Rock een de mount'n,
Fish een de sea,
Dey ent nebbuh bin no nigguh
Wuh tek uh 'ooman f'um me."

LILY: Jedus! 'E gwi' mek Gawd bex wid all ub we!
[*The wind rises to its highest pitch. The Negroes huddle together in terror. They begin to sway and moan.*
CROWN *stands in middle of room, his arms thrown wide. His voice rises aboved the wind.*]

CROWN: Ent you yeddy Gawd A'mighty duh laugh up dey? Dat right, ole Fr'en'! Gawd laugh en' Crown laugh back!
[*Throws back his head and laughs. The wind shrieks above his laugh.*] You luk'um, enty? Uh gib' you anudduh wu'se!
[*Sings*]:
"Uh yent no doctuh,
Needuhso 'e son,
But Uh kin cool you febuh
Ontell de doctuh come."
[*While he is singing, the wind suddenly ceases. The Negroes look at one another, appalled by the suddenness of the change.*]

BESS: De storm mus'e obuh, enty?

PORGY: 'E jis' duh res'. W'en de win' stan'so, 'e gwi' staa't 'gen, wus'den'ebbuh.

CROWN: Ent Uh tell you Gawd luk'um? 'E quiet now fuh liss'n.
[*He bursts again into song*]:
"Uh laugh een de cuntry,
Uh laugh een de town.
'Kase uh cripple t'ink' 'e gwi'
Tek uh 'ooman f'um Crown."

[*Then begins to shuffle.*] Come on, Bess! You ent no Gawd-fayr'n' nigguh. Come on! You nyusetuh be be de bes' dan-cuh een Chaa'stun. Ef you ent wan' dance wid me, mebbe you new man kin dance wid you! Come on, Maria. You cyan' tell me dese.Gawd-fayr'n' 'ooman hab you.
[*Roars with laughter.* BESS *is silent. He dances a few more steps.*] Come on, Maria! You cyan' tell me de Gawd-fayr'n' 'ooman hab you!

[MARIA *hesitates*, CROWN *dances on. Laughs.*] Dis ole lady too fat fuh dance. 'E done fuh fat!

MARIA: [*Indignantly*]: Who dat say Uh done fuh fat?
[*Gets lumberingly to her feet and begins to shuffle.* MINGO *begins to clap for them.*]

CROWN: [*Dancing*]: How 'bout ole Spo't'n' Life?
[SPORTING LIFE *joins in the dancing.* PETER *begins to clap.*]

LILY: Stop dat, you ole fool!

CROWN: [*Dancing near* PETER *and shouting in his ear*]: Dis nigguh too ole fuh dance!

PETER: [*Indignant, puffing out his chest*]: Who dat say Uh too ole? [*Gets laboriously to his feet and begins a feeble shuffle.*]
[*A group are now forgetting their terror in song and dance in the middle of the room. Another group, including* SERENA, *are looking on disapprovingly and with fear in their faces.* CLARA *pays no attention to it all, gazes steadily from window.* PORGY *and* BESS *sit together, absorbed in each other. Every now and then* CROWN *cuts a pigeon wing before* BESS. *She ignores him. He laughs and dances away.*
A wild crescendo shriek cuts across the sound of merriment. The dancers stop in their places. Everyone turns to CLARA, *who is pointing from the window, her eyes wild and horror-stricken. They all rush to the window.* SERENA *and* ANNIE *are already trying to comfort* CLARA.]

ANNIE: 'Co'se uh boat done tu'n obun! 'E ent de Sea Gull!

CLARA: 'E hab red gonnil, samelukkuh de Sea Gull!

SERENA: Ent you know de Sea Gull hab bu'd 'puntop 'e bow wid 'e wing 'pread?

MINGO: [*Pointing*]: 'E gwi' come up obuh yanduh.

SERENA: Shum! 'E ent hab no bu'd! Watch-----
[*She breaks off suddenly with widening eyes.* CLARA *cries out.*]

MINGO: Gawd! 'E de Sea Gull, fuh true!

CLARA: [*Shaking off* SERENA'S *arm*]: Lemme go!

PETER: Weh you gwine?

SERENA. [*Holding her*]: Wait, now, Clara!

CLARA: [*Breaks from* SERENA'S *hold. Runs frantically to the door. Then turns back suddenly to* BESS.] Bess, keep me baby 'tell Uh come back!
[*Thrusts the baby into* BESS'S *arms. Wrests the door open while the Negroes call protests after her.*]

BESS: Don' go, Clara!
[CLARA *rushes out. The door bangs shut behind her. A startled moment of silence. They all stand looking at closed door.*]

MINGO: Dat 'ooman t'ink 'e gwi' fin' Jake 'libe?

BESS: 'E ent right fuh Clara be out dey by 'ese'f!

SPORTING LIFE: Eb'ryt'ing cyaam now!

PORGY: Dat storm gwi' come back enny minute!

BESS: Mek somebody ent gone fuh Clara? Don' lef'um dey by 'ese'f! [*No one moves.*]

SPORTING LIFE: Wuffuh de fool 'ooman gone?

MARIA: Eb'rybody yuh duh chickin, enty?

MINGO: Go yo'se'f, Auntie! Dey ent no wabe big 'nuf fuh drowndid you.

PETER: [*Starting for door*]: Ennybody gwine wid me?

BESS: [*Holding him back*]: You ent gwine, Daddy Petuh. You too ole! [*Looking scornfully over the room*]: Ent dey no man 'roun' yuh?

CROWN: Weh all dem nigguh wuh wan' fuh meet Jedgemunt? Go on! You bin ax fuh sump'n en' you ent hab de gizzut fuh gone git'um! Now you chance!

[*Laughs. Goes and stands before* BESS, *looking sideways to see effect on her.*]
Porgy, Mek you duh set dey? Ent you yeddy you 'ooman call fuh man?

[*Again glances toward* BESS; *then runs to door, throwing up his arms and calling. Calls the men by name:* "Go 'long, Sam!" etc.
Awright, Ole Fr'en' up dey! Us on anudduh bout!
[*Jerks door open and runs out.*]
[*A moment of silence. The stage has grown perceptibly lighter. All the Negroes crowd to the window, looking over each other's shoulders through slats of the closed shutters.*]

PETER: Dey Clara yiz, 'mos' tuh de w'awf, awready!

BESS: De watuh berry deep?

SERENA: 'Mos' tuh 'e was'e!

SPORTING LIFE: Gawd! Crown duh 'plash right t'ru dat watuh!
[*They watch a moment in silence.*
A roar of wind and water. The stage darkens suddenly. With a swift, sucking sound, the shutters fly apart. Confused cries of] "Oh, Jedus hab mussy!" 'Gawd A'mighty! De storm come back!" "Ent uh suh 'e gwi' come back mo' wussuh de ebuh."

SERENA: [*Kneeling centre*]: Gawd duh mek ansuh tuh Crown!
[*Others kneel with her, shrinking close together, moaning with
terror.*]

MINGO: [*At window, his voice rising high in horror*]: Gawd
A'mighty, de w'awf gwine!

BESS: [*Screaming futilely against the wind*]: Clara! Clara!
[*Wild shrieks of horror from all the Negroes at window. Then a
terrific roar, accompanied by the splintering of timber. Then a
sudden awed silence in the room.* PETER *turns the women
from the window, blocking further view. They huddle together
in the centre of the room around* SERENA'S *group.* BESS
crosses to PORGY. *Sits beside him, the baby in her arms. All
the others fall upon their knees as with one accord they begin
to sing the* "Jedgemunt Day Sperritual"
BESS *does not sing, but sits holding the baby close, with a rapt
look in her eyes.*]
"All us gwi' pray tuhgedduh on dat day,
All us gwi' pray tuhgedduh on dat day,
En' Uh gwi' fall 'pun me knee en' face de ris'n' sun
Oh Lawd hab mussy on me!

"Us gwi' drink wine tuhgedduh on dat day,
Us gwi' drink wine tuhgedduh on dat day," etc.

"Us gwi' eat bread tuhgedduh on dat day,
Us gwi' eat bread tuhgedduh on dat day,
En' Uh gwi' fall 'pun me knee en' face de ris'n' sun
Oh, Lawd hab mussy on me!"

DADDY PETER: [*In the midst of the singing*]: Hallylooyuh! Gawd
hab mussy on Crown en' Clara soul.
[BESS *turns and looks directly at* PORGY. *With an expression of
awe in his face, he reaches out a timid hand and touches the
baby's cheek.*

*The roar increases. The shutters fly back and forth. With fear-
stricken eyes, the Negroes sway and pat and sing, their voices
sometimes rising above the roar of the wind and sometimes
drowned by it.*
BESS *continues silent, looking straight ahead of her, tenderness,
yearning, and awe in her face.* PORGY *sits watching her.
The shutters crash more violently. The roar of wind and water
increases. The Negroes huddle closer and sing on.*]

CURTAIN

ACT FOUR

ACT FOUR

Scene One

Chimes. St. Michael's strikes one. Curtain. The court, dark
   except for lights around the closed shutters of a second-story
   room at back left and the glow from MARIA'S *open door.*
PORGY *is at his window but is only vaguely seen in the darkness.*
   He holds the shutters partly closed so as to screen himself,
   while he is able to look out.
From the second-story room comes the sound of a spiritual muf-
   fled by the closed shutters.
Door to stairway at back left opens and SERENA *comes out.*
   Through the open door the spiritual is heard more plainly. It
   is sung by women's voices — a slow, mournful dirge.
"Nelson, Nelson, don' leh you bredduh cundemn you.
Nelson, Nelson, don' leh you bredduh cundemn you.
Way down een dat lonesome grabeyaa'd."

[SERENA *closes door, muffling the chant. She crosses toward her*
   room; sees the light from MARIA'S *door and pauses.*]

SERENA: You still up, Maria? Huccome you ent sing wid we fuh
   de dead een de storm?

MARIA: [*Coming to her doorway*]: Some dese nigguh gwi' sing
   'tell dayclean! Uh too ti'ed wid de clean-up. De storm wash
   me stobe spang 'cross de skreet. En' 'e bruk me haa't fuh
   yeddy de 'ooman moan fuh de mens wuh puhwide'um wid
   bittle en' lubb'n'. All dem fine nyoung mens dead een de
   storm!
[*In lower voice*]: Uh skay'd w'en Uh t'ink 'bout all de sperrit
   duh liss'n 'roun' dis co't tenight.

SERENA: [*Nervously*]: Uh ent hab no pashunt wid you sperrit talk!
[PORGY *softly moves his shutter.* SERENA *starts.*]
Wuh dat!

MARIA: Jis' Porgy duh watch f'um 'e winduh. [*Draws* SERENA *further from* PORGY'S *window and lowers her voice ominously*]: Wuh 'e duh watch fuh?

SERENA: [*Impatiently*]: Uh yent know!

MARIA: 'E bin dey dey all day. 'E yent gone fuh baig, en' 'e yent gone wid Bess fuh sing fuh de dead.

SERENA: Wuh you mek ub dat?

MARIA: Crown dead, enty? [*Lowers voice still further*]: Porgy mus'e t'ink Crown sperrit gwi' come fuh bodduh Bess.
[SERENA *gives a scornful grunt.*] Gawd gib' dat cripple eye fuh see 'nuf t'ing us cyan' see. Ef 'e duh watch fuh sump'n, sump'n dey dey fuh watch!
[BESS, *the baby in her arms, opens door at left back. The spiritual is again heard clearly.* BESS *does not close door, but stands listening, holding baby close.* MARIA *and* SERENA *move over to listen.*]

WOMEN'S VOICES: "Jake, Jake, don' leh you bredduh cundemn you,
Jake, Jake, don' leh you bredduh cundemn you. ..."

BESS: Dey duh sing fuh Jake en' Clara! Uh jis' cyan' stay!
[*The three women listen a moment in silence.*]

VOICES: "Clara, Clara, don' leh you sistuh cundemn you way down een dat lonesome grabeyaa'd."
[BESS *softly closes door, muffling the singing. Turns toward her own door.*]

SERENA: Wuh us gwi' do wid Clara po' baby?

BESS: [*Stopping short. Turns slowly back*]: Wuh you duh talk 'bout? Clara done come back?

SERENA: [*Looking fearfully about her*]: Wuh you duh talk 'bout?

BESS: Clara mus'e come back en' say sump'n' Uh yent yeddy 'bout. Clara tell me mus' keep dis baby 'tell 'e come back.

SERENA: Somebody haffuh mek sho' de po' chile git raise dees-tunt!

BESS: Clara yent suh nutt'n' 'bout dat, en' 'tell 'e do uh gwi' stan' on 'e las' wu'd en' keep dis baby!
[*Again starts toward her door. Again turns back impulsively.*]: Oh, lemme 'lone, Serena! Cyan' you see Uh yent de same 'ooman wuh nyuse'tuh run wid Crown? Gawd leh Clara gib' me dis baby 'kase 'E know Uh done change. 'E gib' me Porgy 'kase 'E wan' me fuh hab me chance.

[*Looking down at baby*]: Shum! 'E done awready t'ink Uh 'e Ma. Uh too happy dis day! Shum, Serena---hol'um uh minit. Tell'um 'e hab uh good Ma wuh gwi' stan' by'um!
[*Holds baby out to SERENA.*]

[SERENA *takes the baby reluctantly, but responds when it touches her bosom. She rocks it in her arms.*]

SERENA: Yaas, Uh 'spose you hab a good Ma wuh fin'lly at las' hab Gawd een 'e haa't. You ent haffuh fret.
[*Hands baby back to* BESS, *who draws it close.*]

BESS: Shum, Serena, how 'e duh settle down? Dis baby done fuh know 'e home.
[*Turns to go.*]

SERENA: Good-night, Sistuh.
[BESS *pauses slightly, as though taken by surprise.*]

BESS: Good-night, Sistuh.
[*Goes into her room. A dim light appears in the room. The shutters are closed from within.*

SERENA *goes to her room.* MARIA *begins to shut up her shop for the night. Several women carrying lanterns come from the funeral room, leaving the door open. They go out of the gate. The spiritual is again heard.*]

THE SINGERS: "Ummmmm, Ummmmm, yeddy ole Eejup duh howl way down een dat lonesome grabeyaa'd.
"Crown, Crown, don' leh you bredduh cundemn you."
[*There is a sudden raucous laugh in the darkness.* MARIA *starts; then turns and peers into the shadows under* SERENA'S *stairs.*]

MARIA: You low down skunk! Wuffuh you duh hide 'roun' yuh?

SPORTING LIFE: [*Sauntering into the light from* MARIA'S *window*]: Uh jis' duh liss'n tuh de sing'n'. Dat uh nice, happy chune. Dem duh sto' me ole fr'en' Crown, now. [*Laughs again.*]
[MARIA *crosses quickly; closes the door, muffling the singing.*]

MARIA: [*Returning to* SPORTING LIFE]: You ent hab no shame--- You duh laugh at dem po' 'ooman duh sing fuh dem mens!

SPORTING LIFE: Uh ent see no need fuh mek fuss obuh dead mens. W'en uh gal man done gone, dey 'nuf libe mens fuh lub uh good-look'n' gal.

MARIA: Uh know you ent attuh dem gal. You cyan' see Bess ent hab no nyuse fuh you? You ent shum hab uh man?

SPORTING LIFE: Uh see mo'nuh dat, Auntie. [*Laughs as though at a joke all his own.*]

MARIA: Wuh you mean?

SPORTING LIFE: Uh shum hab two mens---w'en uh 'ooman hab two mens, tuhreckly 'e yent hab no mens!

MARIA: [*Threateningly*]: Wuh you mean---Bess hab two mens?

SPORTING LIFE: W'ymekso you t'ink Crown dead?

MARIA: Ent us shum wash 'way wid de w'awf?

SPORTING LIFE: En' ent 'e tell you dat Gawd 'e fr'en'?

MARIA: [*Alarmed*]: You duh tell me Crown ent dead?

SPORTING LIFE: [*Nonchalantly*]: Uh yent tell you nutt'n', Auntie.

MARIA: [*Advancing on him threateningly*]: Yaas, you iz! You gwi' tell me eb'ryt'ing you know dam' quick! [*Corners him.*]

SPORTING LIFE: 'Co'se 'e dead! Ent us yeddy'um duh sing 'e fun' rul song?

MARIA: [*Grabbing his arm and bringing her face close to his*]: You shum, enty?

SPORTING LIFE: Uh cyan' shum ef 'e dead! Mus'e 'e sperrit duh heng 'roun' yuh!

MARIA: [*Meditatively*]: You shum fuh true [*Menacingly*]: Well, ef Bess hab two men, dat sho' count you out!

[SPORTING LIFE *laughs at her. While they talk,* PORGY'S *shutter opens inch by inch.*]

SPORTING LIFE: Dat weh Uh come een! W'en uh 'ooman hab one man, 'e hab'um fuh good. W'en 'e hab two mens, uh kill'n' fuh hab, en' de poleece gwi' tek de leab'n'.

MARIA: [*Warningly*]: Nobody een dis co't gwi' gib' nigguh 'way tuh de poleece.

SPORTING LIFE: 'E stan'so, Auntie! But dem poleece berry smaa't, en' dem gwi' look see kin dey fin' Crown. W'en dey fin'um, tell Bess dat leetle ole Spo't'n' Life stillyet right yuh.

MARIA: [*Starting for him*]: Stillyet you sho' ent gwi' stay berry long tuh dis place!

SPORTING LIFE: [*Hurriedly withdrawing, but not forgetting his swagger*]: 'E awright, ole lady, Uh gwine!
[*Saunters toward gate.*]
[MARIA *turns back to the closing of her shop.* SPORTING LIFE *glances at her over his shoulder. Sees her engaged in barring her windows. Steps swiftly into the darkness under* SERENA'S *stairs.* MARIA *finishes her work. Looks about court. Sees it apparently empty. Goes into her shop. Locks door.*]
[*A child's whimper is heard from* BESS'S *room, then* BESS'S *voice singing in the darkness.*]
"Hush leetle baby, don' you cry,
Hush leetle baby, don' you cry,
Hush leetle baby, don' you cry,
Murruh en' farruh bawn tuh die."

"Uh yeddy t'unduh een de sky,
Uh yeddy t'unduh een de sky,
Uh yeddy t'unduh een de sky,
Mus'e Jedus duh pass by."

"Yeddy uh rumble een de groun',
Yeddy uh rumble een de groun',
Yeddy uh rumble een de groun',
Mus'e de debble duh tu'n 'roun'.

"Hush leetle baby, don' you cry,
Murruh en' farruh bawn tuh die."

[*Her voice trails off sleepily and is silent. During her lullaby, the last singers have come from the funeral room and crossed to their own rooms or gone out at gate. The light in the funeral room goes out.* MARIA'S *light goes out.*
A moment of complete darkness and silence in Catfish Row; then the sudden flash of a match in the darkness reveals SPORT-ING LIFE about to light a cigarette. He hears something at gate and hurriedly extinguishes match, with cigarette unlit.*]

*Against the gray background beyond the gate a gigantic figure can
been seen. The gate opens very slowly and noiselessly.* CROWN
*comes stealthily into court; very gently closes gate behind him.
Picks his way slowly and silently across court. Stops to listen.
Silence. Goes on to* PORGY'S *door. Again listens. Puts his
hand on knob and softly tries door. Opens it very cautiously,
inch by inch. When it is wide enough, he stealthily slips
through. Inch by inch, the door closes.*
A full minute of absolute silence. MARIA *is in her wrapper; opens
her door and stands listening. Satisfied, she is turning back.
A muffled thud sounds from* PORGY'S *room.* MARIA *stops short.
Stands motionless. Suddenly* PORGY'S *laugh is heard, deep,
swelling, lustful. The baby cries out.*]

BESS: [*Within room. Horror in her voice*]: Fuh Gawd sake,
Porgy! Wuh you duh laugh 'bout?

PORGY: [*Triumphantly*]: 'E awright, honey. You ent haffuh
worry no mo'. You hab Porgy now, en' 'e gwi' tek cyah 'e
'ooman. Ent Uh done tell you you hab uh man now?
[MARIA *crosses the court swiftly. Opens* PORGY'S *door, goes in and
closes it behind her.*
Again the flash of a match in the shadows. SPORTING LIFE *lights
his cigarette and continues his vigil.*]

CURTAIN

Scene Two

*St. Michael's chimes and strikes six. The curtain rises on the
court, silent and apparently deserted.*
*After a moment, three white men appear outside the gate. One is
the* DETECTIVE *who arrested* PETER. *The second is the* CORO-
NER, *a fat, easy-going, florid man. The third is a* POLICE-
MAN.

DETECTIVE: [*To* POLICEMAN, *pointing off right*]: Bring the
wagon 'round to the corner, Al, and wait for us there.
[*The* POLICEMAN *goes off right. The* DETECTIVE *and* CORONER
come in at gate.]
This is the joint. I'd like to get something on it this time that
would justify closing it up as a public nuisance and turning
the lot of 'em into the street. It's alive with crooked niggers.

CORONER: [*Looking around him*]: Looks pretty dead to me.

DETECTIVE: Dead, hell! If you was on the force, 'stead of sit-
ting down in the coroner's office, you'd know we don't
make a move that isn't watched by a hundred pair of eyes.
[*The* CORONER *looks exceedingly uncomfortable. Glances appre-
hensively about him.*]
There! Did you catch that?
[*Points at a window.* CORONER *starts.*]
They're gone now.

CORONER: Don't know as I have much business, after all. Just
to get a witness to identify the body at the inquest. Maybe
you'll bring one along for me when you come.

DETECTIVE: Like hell I will! You stay and get your own witness,
and I'll learn you something about handling niggers, too.
Now, let's see — got several leads here! The widow of Robbins, the fellow Crown killed. That's her room there. And
then there's the corpse's woman. She's living with the cripple in there now.

CORONER: What makes you think the buck was killed here?

DETECTIVE: [*Pointing toward sea*]: Found right out there.

CORONER: Found at flood tide. Might have been washed in from
miles out.

DETECTIVE: A hell of a lot you know about niggers. Come on!
I'll show you.

[CORONER *nods and follows* DETECTIVE. *They stop at door leading to* SERENA'S *room.* DETECTIVE *kicks it open, and shouts up the stairs.*]

DETECTIVE: Come on down, Serena Robbins, and make it damn quick!

[*There is silence for a moment, then the shutters of* SERENA'S *window are slowly opened, and* ANNIE *looks out.*]

ANNIE: Fuh de t'ree day Serena bin sick een de bed, en' Uh duh set yuh wid'um.

DETECTIVE: The hell she has! Tell her, if she don't come down, I'll get the wagon and run her in.

ANNIE: 'E cyan' lef' 'e bed, boss. 'E sick tuh dat!

DETECTIVE: She'll leave it damn quick if she knows what's good for her.

[ANNIE *disappears. A loud moaning is heard. Then* ANNIE *reappears accompanied by another woman. Between them they support* SERENA. *She wears a voluminous white nightgown, and her face and head are bound in a towel. She collapses across the window sill with a loud groan.*]

Drop that racket!

[SERENA *is silent.*]

SERENA: [*Slowly and as though in great pain*]: Uh bin yuh sick 'een dis bed fuh de t'ree day en' de t'ree night.

ANNIE: Us binnuh set yuh wid'um eenjurin' de t'ree day en' de t'ree night.

THE OTHER WOMAN: Dat de Gawd trute!

CORONER: Would you swear to that?

SERENA, ANNIE, and OTHER WOMAN: [*In unison, as though answer had been learned by rote*]: Yaas, boss, us swaytogawd!

CORONER: [*To* DETECTIVE]: There you are — an airtight alibi.
[DETECTIVE *regards* CORONER *with scorn.*]

DETECTIVE: [*To* SERENA]: You know damn well you were out
yesterday. I've a good mind to send for the wagon and carry
you in.
[*The women are silent.* DETECTIVE *waits, then shouts abruptly*]:
Well?

THE THREE WOMEN: [*Again in unison*]: Us swagtogawd us bin
een dis room fuh t'ree day.

DETECTIVE: [*Bluffing*]: Ah-hh, that's what I wanted! So you
swear you were in last night, eh?
[*The women are frightened and silent.*]
And just two months ago — right here — Crown killed your
husband, didn't he?
[*No answer.*]
Answer me!
[DETECTIVE *runs halfway upstairs.*]
You'll either talk here or in jail. Get that! Did Crown kill Rob-
bins? Yes or no!
[SERENA *nods her head.*]
Exactly. And last night Crown got his right here — didn't he?
[*Women are silent except* SERENA, *who groans as though in pain.*
DETECTIVE *pretends to construe groan as assent — trium-
phantly.*]
Yes, and how do you know he was killed if you didn't see it?

WOMEN: [*In unison*]: Us ent see nutt'n', boss. Us bin yuh de
t'ree day en' night, en' de winduh bin shet!

DETECTIVE: [*Shouting*]: Look at me, Robbins! Do you mean to
tell me that the man who killed your husband was bumped
off right here, under your window, and you didn't know?

WOMEN: [*In unison*]: Us ent see nutt'n', boss. Us bin yuh-----

DETECTIVE: [*Interrupting*]: — three days and nights, with the window closed. You needn't do that one again. [*Turning away disgustedly*]: Oh, hell! You might as well argue with a parrot cage, but you'll never break them without your own witnesses, and you'll never get 'em.

[*The three women leave the window, closing shutters.*]
Well, come along. Let's see what's here. [Goes to LILY'S *and* PETER'S *door. Throws it open.*]
Come on out here, you!
[LILY *comes to door.*]
What's your name?

LILY: [*Seeing* CORONER]: Do, Lawd, ef 'e ent Mistuh Jennin'!

CORONER: Well, Lily! So you live here? [*To* DETECTIVE]: I'll answer for this woman. She worked for us for years.

DETECTIVE: That don't prove she don't know anything about this murder, does it? [*To* LILY]: What's your name?

LILY: [*Stubbornly*]: Uh yent know nutt'n' 'bout'um!

DETECTIVE: [*Shouting at her*]: I didn't ask you whether —

CORONER: Let me question her. [*Kindly to* LILY]: What's your name?

LILY: Do, Mistuh Jennin'! Me name stillyet Lily Ho'me.

CORONER: I know your name was Lily Holmes, but you left us to get married. What's your name now?

LILY: Lawd, Mistuh Jennin', Uh de same Lily Ho'me! You t'ink Uh gwi' tek enny ole nigguh name? En' Uh yent gwi' ge'm me name needuh.

DETECTIVE: [*Looking through door*]: That your husband?
[*Calling into room*]: Come on out here, you!

LILY: Uh gwi' fetch'um. [*Goes into room. Returns with* PETER.]

CORONER: Why, it's the old honey man!
[PETER is terror-stricken at sight of DETECTIVE.]

DETECTIVE: [*Recognizing him*]: Oh, so it's you, is it? Well,
Uncle, do you want to go back to jail or are you going to
come clean?

LILY: [*Appealing to* CORONER]: No need fuh you ax'um nutt'n'
een de fus' place, 'e deef, en' een de two place 'e rectify
een 'e min'.

CORONER: But, Lily, you didn't marry the old honey man?

LILY: [*Surveying* PETER]: Wuh wrong wid'um?

CORONER: He's not a suitable age.

LILY: [*Puzzled*]: Wuh dat 'e yent?

CORONER: Do you think he's the right age?

LILY: Sho' 'e de right age! 'E aighty-two!

CORONER: An old man like that's apt to linger on your hands.
[DADDY PETER, *hearing nothing of conversation, but feeling that
he is its subject, is nodding and smiling with self-
appreciation.*]

LILY: No, boss! Ef uh marri'd uh nyoung man en' 'e tek sick,
mebbe 'e linguh on me han'. [*Points to* PETER, *who smiles
more amiably.*] But 'e yent gwi' linguh. Ef Petuh tek sick,
'e gwine!

CORONER: What did you marry him for?

LILY: Well, boss, 'e stan' so. You 'membuh dem fit ub de mis'ry
Uh nyuse'tuh hab een de nighttime? De doctuh say, "Lily
Ho'me, some dese night you gwi' dead een you bed by
you'se'f." So Uh figguh Uh bes' marri'd dat nigguh eeduhso
Uh gwi' dead by me'se'f. Sence Uh marri'd'um, do' Uh ent
hab no mo' mis'ry, en' Uh ent hab no mo' nyuse fuh de
nigguh.

DETECTIVE: [*To* CORONER]: Say, are you investigating a murder or just paying social calls? [*To* LILY *and* PETER]: That'll do for you two. Get inside.
[LILY *and* PETER *hurriedly return to their room.*]

CORONER: Well, seems to me I get as much out of them as you do.

DETECTIVE: Come on, let's put the cripple and his woman through. I have a hunch that's where we'll find our bacon.
[*Crosses toward* PORGY'S *door.* CORONER *follows.*]

CORONER: All right. Go ahead. I'm watching you handle them.

DETECTIVE: You won't find the cripple much of a witness. I tried to break him in the Robbins case but he wouldn't come through. [*Kicks the door open with a bang.*] Come on out, both of you niggers. Step lively now!
[BESS *helps* PORGY *to seat on doorstep. Then she stands by him, the baby in her arms.* DETECTIVE *enters room.*]

CORONER: [*To* PORGY]: What is your name?
[PORGY *looks at him keenly, then, reassured, smiles.*]

PORGY: Jis' Porgy. You know me, boss. You done gimme 'nuffuh penny tuh Meet'n' Skreet.

CORONER: Of course! You're the goat man. I didn't know you without your wagon. Now, this nigger Crown — you knew him by sight, didn't you?

PORGY: [*As though remembering with difficulty*]: Yaas, boss, uh 'membuhr'um. 'E nyuse'tuh come yuh long time ago.

CORONER: You could identify him, I suppose.
[PORGY *looks blank.*]
You'd know him if you saw him again, I mean.

PORGY: [*Slowly*]: Yaas, boss, ef Uh shum! [*With dawning apprehension*]: But Uh sho' ent wan' shum!

[CORONER *laughs. Makes note in notebook. Puts it in pocket. Calls to* DETECTIVE.]

CORONER: Well, I'm through. Let's pull freight.

DETECTIVE: [*Appears in doorway; looks knowingly at* PORGY *and* BESS]: Mighty clean floor in there. Funny it got its first scrubbing in twenty years this morning.

BESS: Uh scrub me flo' eb'ry week. You kin ax deseyuh people 'bout dat!

DETECTIVE: [*Sneering*]: Oh, yes! More witnesses! *[Then triumphantly*]: But you missed the blood under the bed this time. *[Jerks out his gun, covers* PORGY, *shouts*]: Come, out with it! You killed Crown, didn't you? Speak up, or I'll hang you sure as hell!
[PORGY *and* BESS *sit silent, with eyes lowered.*]
Well?

BESS: Uh yent onduhstan', boss. Dey ent no blood 'neet' de bed, en' nobody ent kill Crown 'een we room.

CORONER: [*Drawing* DETECTIVE *aside*]: For God's sake, Duggan, let's call it a day. The cripple couldn't kill a two-hundred-pound buck and tote him a hundred yards.

DETECTIVE: You don't know much about niggers, do you?

CORONER: [*Turning toward gate*]: Anyway, I'm through, and I've got to get along. It's 'most time for my inquest.
[BESS *and* PORGY *go swiftly inside. Close door.*]

DETECTIVE: [*Following* CORONER *reluctantly*]: Got your witness?

CORONER: Yeh.
[*They go out gate and off to left.*
Again the court is deserted and silent. For a moment, there is no sound or movement.
Then, in one of the rooms, a voice is raised singing]

"Ent it haa'd tuh be uh nigguh!
Ent it haa'd tuh be uh nigguh!"
[*Another voice joins, then another. In a moment, the empty court
is ringing with the song, sung mockingly, triumphantly.
Another moment, and doors and shutters begin to fly open. The
Negroes come from their doors or lean from their windows,
and the court is quickly filled with life and movement. They
are all singing.*
SERENA'S *door flies open, and she comes out singing. She is fully
dressed and carries a great basket of clothes, which she
begins to hang on line while she sings.*
BESS *helps* PORGY *on to the doorstep and sits beside him, the baby
in her arms. Both are singing.* LILY *comes out carrying the
honey tray.* PETER *follows. She balances it on his head.*
SCIPIO *drives* PORGY'S *goat cart in through archway.
Then someone breaks into a wilder tune, and all the others
instantly change to the new song.*]
"Seddown! Uh cyan' seddown!
Seddown! Uh cyan' seddown!
Me soul dat happy Uh cyan' seddown!"
[*A Negro near the gate looks out, suddenly gives a loud hiss and
waves his arms — in a warning gesture.
The song ceases abruptly.* SERENA *grabs her wash from the line.
The Negroes return swiftly and silently to their rooms. Doors
and shutters close stealthily.*
BESS *attempts to help* PORGY *to his feet, but, seeing that they have
no time, he sinks down again on his doorstep and pretends to
doze.* BESS *goes inside, closes door.* SCIPIO *drives the goat
back through archway.
The court is again silent, and deserted by all but* PORGY.
A POLICEMAN *enters from left. Comes in at gate. Looks about
court. Sees* PORGY, *who is apparently oblivious of him.
Crosses to* PORGY.]

POLICEMAN: Hey, you!

[PORGY *opens his eyes.*]

You're Porgy, aren't you? I've got something for you.

[Holds out paper. PORGY *looks at it in alarm.* POLICEMAN *speaks kindly.*]

You needn't be afraid to take it. It's just a summons as a witness at the coroner's inquest. All you've got to do is view the body and tell the coroner who it is.

[PORGY *is suddenly terror-stricken. His voice shakes.*]

PORGY: Uh haffuh look 'pun Crown face?

POLICEMAN: Yes, that's all.

PORGY: Wid all de w'ite folk, dem, duh watch me?

POLICEMAN: Oh, cheer up! I reckon you've seen a dead nigger before. It'll be all over in a few minutes.

[BESS *appears in doorway, listening, her eyes wide with horror.*]

PORGY: Dey ent gwi' be no nigguh een dat room 'cep'n' me?

POLICEMAN: Just you and Crown — if you still call him one. [*Turns away.*]

PORGY: [*Scarcely able to speak for terror*]: Boss, Uh kin jis' bring uh 'ooman 'long? Uh kin bring me 'ooman?

POLICEMAN: [*Slightly impatient*]: No, you can't bring anyone. Say, you're the cripple, aren't you? I'll get the wagon and carry you down. And as soon as you've seen Crown, you can come home. [*Starts for gate.*]

PORGY: [*Desperately*]: Boss-----

POLICEMAN: Now, listen, I've summoned you, and you've got to go, or it's contempt of court. I'll call the wagon for you. [*Goes out gate and off to left.*]

[*As soon as he has gone, doors open stealthily. The Negroes come out and gather about* PORGY, *speaking in low, frightened tones.*]

PORGY: Oh, Gawd! Wuh Uh gwi' do?

BESS: You haffuh gone! Mebbe you kin call you'se'f duh look 'pun'um, en' sametime shet you eye.

MARIA: You gwi' be awright, Porgy. You jis' duh witness.

SPORTING LIFE: Un ent so sho' ub dat!
[*They all look at him in alarm.*]
Uh yent know who kill Crown. 'Cep'n' Uh know w'en de man who do'um look 'puntop'um, Crown woun' gwi' bleed.

PORGY: [*Terror-stricken*]: Oh, Jedus!

SPORTING LIFE: Dat he'p de poleece fuh know who done'um!

PORGY: [*In a panic, moaning*]: Uh cyan' look 'pun 'e face! Oh, Gawd! Wuh Uh gwi' do?

SPORTING LIFE: [*Taking command of the situation*]: Liss'n tuh me! Do wuh Uh say en' you ent haffuh look on 'e face.

PORGY: Wuh Uh mus' do?

SPORTING LIFE: Mek'ace oonuh nigguh! Us haffuh git Porgy out ub yuh! Scipio, git de goat! Mingo, come'yuh en' he'p me wid Porgy!

BESS: Don' go, Porgy! You cyan' git'way!

SPORTING LIFE: 'E haffuh git'way, eeduhso 'e gwi' heng, fuh true!

PORGY: [SCIPIO *has brought the goat cart.* SPORTING LIFE *and* MINGO *are lifting* PORGY *in while he moans with terror and mutters unintelligibly.*]

SPORTING LIFE: Porgy, lean fuh Bedun Alley! W'en you git dey, tu'n een en' lay low!

MINGO: Bedun Alley stan' fudduh. 'E cyan' git dey dey!

SPORTING LIFE: Shet'up, Mingo! Uh know wuffuh do! Awright, Porgy, light out!

MARIA: Mek'ace, staa't'um!

BESS: Mek de goat run! Twis' 'e tail!

[*The clang of the patrol wagon bell is heard approaching rapidly. The Negroes stand as though paralyzed with terror.*]

MINGO: Dey done git yuh!

BESS: Oh, Gawd! 'E too late!

SPORTING LIFE: No, 'e yent! Come leh we git'um out yuh!

[*Directs them to the archway. They drive the goat through, then mass in front of archway, hiding* PORGY *from view.*

SPORTING LIFE *saunters across the court as though he had nothing to do with the affair, and awaits developments.*

The patrol bell rings more slowly as the wagon slows down, then comes to a stop at left of gate just out of view.

The POLICEMAN *again comes in at gate. Looks toward* PORGY'S *door. Crosses to it abruptly. Throws it open.*]

POLICEMAN: Hey, you there! [*Runs to gate. Calls.*] Jim! The fool's trying to make a get-away! Come on! [*Turns to the Negroes.*] Where did he go?

[*They look at him with blank faces.*]

All right! [*Starts for* PORGY'S *door.*]

[*The* SECOND POLICEMAN *enters from left.*]

You take that side, Jim. I'll take this. [*Goes into* PORGY'S *room.*]

[SECOND POLICEMAN *goes through* SERENA'S *door. As soon as both* POLICEMEN *are out of sight, the Negroes beckon to* PORGY, *who drives from archway and quickly toward gate. The shutters of an upper window are thrown open, and the* FIRST POLICEMAN *looks out.*]

POLICEMAN: Hey, you! What d'you think you're doing?

[PORGY *leans forward and wrings the goat's tail. The astonished animal leaps forward and goes out gate at a run.*]

Jim!

[*The* SECOND POLICEMAN *throws open shutters of room opposite and leans from window.*]

Look there! [*Points to* PORGY *as he disappears off left.*]
[*Both* POLICEMEN *burst into peals of laughter.*
The Negroes follow to gate, pushing it shut, looking out through
bars.]

SECOND POLICEMAN: He must want to have a race.
[*The two* POLICEMEN *leave the windows and a minute later come*
running from doors.]

FIRST POLICEMAN: Racing the wagon! That's good!
[*They start toward gate.*]

SECOND POLICEMAN: [*Laying a hand on the other's arm:*] Say,
   let him get a start.
[*They double up with laughter.*]
This is going to be good!

FIRST POLICEMAN: Here, you niggers, Get away from the gate.
[*The Negroes stand back. He opens gate.*]
Come on now! We're off!
[*They run out gate, still shouting with laughter. They run off*
right. The Negroes press close about gate to watch.
The clang of the patrol wagon bell is heard as the vehicle sets off
at top speed.]
ANNIE: Oh, Gawd! Dey gwi' git'um fuh sho'!
MARIA: Ef 'e kin jis' tu'n de cawnuh!
LILY: Mebbe dey cyan' fin'um!
BESS: [*Turning hopelessly away*]: Dey ent no use!
[*The tension in the crowd of watchers suddenly relaxes, and their*
faces assume hopeless expressions.]
Dey got'um?

LILY: Yaas, dey got'um!

SERENA: Dey duh pit Porgy en' de goat, alltwo, een de waggin.
[BESS *sits hopelessly on her doorstep. The other Negroes return to*
their various rooms and tasks. SPORTING LIFE *saunters*
across court and sits down on step by BESS.
The stage is darkening. A light appears in a window.]

BESS: Oh, Gawd! Dey gwi' cya'um fuh look 'pun Crown face!

SPORTING LIFE: [*Laughing*]: No, dey ent, Sistuh. Dat nigguh ent no witness now. Dey gwi' lock'um up!

MINGO: [*At gate*]: Dat de trute! Dey done tu'n de waggin 'roun' en' gone tuh de jail!

BESS: Well, dat mo'bettuh den 'e look 'pun Crown! [*Fearfully*]: Fuh how long 'e gwi' lock'up?

SPORTING LIFE: [*Sympathetically*]: Not fuh long! 'Bout uh yeah!

BESS: Uh yeah?

SPORTING LIFE: Contemp' ub co't---dat uh berry bad chaa'ge! [BESS *drops her face into her hands.*]
Jis' lukkuh Uh done tell you. Nobody home now but Bess en' ole Spo't'n' Life!

BESS: Uh ent hab no time fuh you!

SPORTING LIFE: [*Laughing*]: Sho' you hab! You hab nice wacashun fuh play 'roun' wid you ole fr'en'. Contemp' ub co't uh berry bad chaa'ge! Dat nigguh ent gwi' git; back fuh uh yeah.

BESS: [*Alarmed*]: Fuh true, Spo't'n' Life? Dey gwi' lock'um up fuh uh yeah?

SPORTING LIFE: Uh yeah, fuh sho'. Come'yuh, Sistuh gib' me you han'.
[*He takes her hand. She is too preoccupied to resist.*]
Old Spo't'n' Life hab de stuff fuh tek'way de lonesome blues! [*Pours powder into her hand.* BESS *looks down at it.*]

BESS: Happy dus'! [*Gazes at the powder with fascinated horror.*] Uh tell you Uh yent wan' none dat stuff!

SPORTING LIFE: 'E ent 'nuf fuh hu't uh flea!

BESS: Uh yent wan' dis stuff, nigguh! [*But she continues to hold it in her hand.*]

SPORTING LIFE: Dis' uh leetle tetch fuh ole 'time sake!
[BESS *suddenly claps her hand over her face. When she takes it away, it is empty.* SPORTING LIFE *smiles with satisfaction.*]
Ent dat de t'ing? En' 'membuh plenty mo' weh dat come f'um! Uh gwine tuh New Yawk tuhmorruh mawnin'.
[*Pauses significantly.* BESS *says nothing.*] Mek you so fool. Wuh you gwi' do yuh fuh uh yeah? Now you chance!
[BESS *leaps to her feet, her eyes blazing. She glares at* SPORTING LIFE *with contempt and hatred.*]

BESS: You low down houn', git 'way f'um me do'! Lef' um, you rattlesnake! Dat wuh you iz! Rattlesnake!
[*While she berates him,* SPORTING LIFE *lights a cigarette, continues to sit on step.*]

SPORTING LIFE: You kin onrabble you mout', Sistuh. Uh gwi' be right yuh w'en you wan' dat nex' shot!
[BESS *runs suddenly past him into her room. Slams door behind her.* SPORTING LIFE *sits smiling to himself and leisurely blowing smoke rings.*
[MARIA *comes to her doorway. Sees him. Crosses to him.*]

MARIA: [*Contemptuously*]: Wuffuh you duh wait 'roun' yuh?

SPORTING LIFE: [*Smokes contentedly.*] Jis' wait'n'!

MARIA: Wuh you t'ink you gwi' git?

SPORTING LIFE: [*With shrug of shoulders*]: Ummmmmmmm---jis' wait'n'!

MARIA: [*Turning scornfully away*]: You mus'e ent know Bess! [*Recrosses to her shop.*]
[SPORTING LIFE *watches her till she has reached her doorstep.*]

SPORTING LIFE: [*In a low voice, not intended for* MARIA *to hear*]: You mus'e ent know Happy Dus'
[MARIA *does not hear. Goes into shop; closes door.* SPORTING LIFE *continues to wait. St. Michael's chimes the half hour.*]

CURTAIN

Scene Three

Chimes. Two o'clock. The court is as usual, except that PORGY'S
*door and shutters are closed. Negroes are coming and going
about their tasks.*
PETER, LILY, *and* MINGO *sit at* MARIA'S *table. She is busy serving
them.* SCIPIO *is playing near the gate.* SERENA *sits near her
door rocking a baby in her arms and singing, "Hush leetle
baby, don' you cry."* MARIA *goes into her shop.*
PORGY *drives up outside the gate and calls softly to* SCIPIO. *His
air is one of mystery.*

PORGY: Scipio, Porgy back home! Op'n de gate, en' don' mek
no nize.
[SCIPIO *goes reluctantly to gate, opens it, and leads the goat
inside.* SERENA *looks up, sees* PORGY, *stops singing in the
middle of a bar, and hunches over the baby as though to hide
it.*
*Various Negroes about the court look up, see him, and go silently
into their rooms.*
PORGY *is too preoccupied with his secret to notice anything. He
drives over and stops beside* MARIA'S *table.* LILY, PETER, *and*
MINGO *half rise, then see that it is too late to escape, and
resume their seats.*]

PORGY: [*In a joyous but guarded voice*]: Don' nobody leh Bess
know Uh back, 'tell Uh ready. Uh hab 'sprize fuhr'um!
[*He does not notice that the others are silent and embarrassed,
and, reaching into the wagon, commences to remove pack-
ages, talking volubly all the time. He unwraps a harmonica
and hands it to* SCIPIO.]
Yuh, boy! T'row'way dat ole mout' awgun en' staa' een on dis
one! See de pitchuh ub de brass ban' on' um? Fus' news
you know, you gwi' be play'n' wid de offun ban'!
[*He turns to* LILY]: Yuh, gal, hol'up you head. Uh yent nebbuh
luk dem ole fun'rul bonnet Petuh buy fuh you. Pit'um on en'
mek all de Red Bu'd en' Blue jay jallus!

[*Unwraps a gorgeous, feather-trimmed hat and hands it to her.*]

[LILY *takes hat, but is unable to speak her thanks.* PORGY *is hurrying on, and does not notice this. He opens a package and shakes out a gay dress, then lays it on the table.*]

Now, dis de style fuh Bess! 'E one gal wuh look good een red dress. [*He opens a hat and places it beside the dress.*] Uh 'spose Uh de fus' nigguh 'roun' yuh wuh gone jail po' en' lef'um rich! Porgy luck bin ride high. Nutt'n cyan' stop'um! W'en de buckruh saa'ch me een jail, Uh hab me lucky bone een me mout'. En' w'en Uh get settle een me new bo'd'n'-house, Uh gone right t'ru dem odduh crap'shoot'n' nigguh luk Glory Hallylooyuh!

[*He takes a package from the cart, opens it, and holds up a baby dress.*] Now ent dis de t'ing? 'Co'se de baby ent dat laa'ge fuh weh'um yet. But 'e duh grow fas' 'e gwi' be een'um 'fo' fus' fros'!

[*Continues his story.*]

Yaas, suh! Dem bone ent fuh stop! Dey gone skrate t'ru dat jail, en' cya' me 'long'um! Den de las' day, big buckruh gyaa'd yeddy 'bout'um en' 'e come suh Uh haffuh gib'up de bone. 'Cep' Uh bin shum tuh de watch house, duh roll bone wid de jailuh, en' Uh know weh 'e lib! Uh ax dat buckruh ef 'e wan' me fuh show'um huffuh sing lucky tuh de bone 'fo' Uh g'em up. 'Fo' 'e kin git'way, Uh done tek'um fuh t'ree dolluh en' seb'n cent, en' dishyuh shu't!

[*He proudly exhibits shirt that he is wearing. His purchases are now all spread out on the table, and he looks from them to the faces of the Negroes.*]

Now de time fuh call Bess. Bess, you Porgy duh home!

[*There is a moment of absolute silence.* LILY *gets to her feet, buries her face in her hands, and runs to her room.* PETER *starts to follow.* MINGO *rises and goes toward* MARIA'S *door.*]

Lily, Petuh, Mingo, weh oonuh gwine? Wuh kind'uh dam' wel-
come dis fuh uh man wuh bin een jail fuh uh week, en' fuh
cuntemp' ub co't at dat! Oh, yaas, you ent haffuh min' 'bout
me en' Bess! Us alltime wan' we fr'en' wid we!

[*They continue to withdraw. He looks about him in growing surprise, and discovers* SERENA *hunched up silently over the
baby.*]

Serena, you sho' wu'k fas', Sistuh. Uh yent bin gone uh week,
en' you done hab chile!

[SERENA *rises hurriedly, exposing baby for first time.*]

Hol' on! Lemme see dat chile. Dat Bess baby, enty? Huccome
you duh min'um? Weh Bess iz? Mek'um ent come w'en un
call'um?

SERENA: [*Calling*]: Come'yuh, Maria! Porgy duh home! You
haffuh come talk wid'um.

[PORGY *drives to his own door.*]

PORGY: Weh you iz, Bess? You ent dey dey?

[MARIA *comes to her doorway.* PORGY *turns to her, his eyes wide
with alarm.*]

Weh Bess?

[MARIA *sits on her doorstep.* PORGY *turns his goat and drives over
to her.*]

Mek'ace, Maria, tell me weh Bess!

[MARIA *does not answer.*]

Fuh Gawd sake! Weh 'e iz?

MARIA: [*Trying to put on a bold face*]: Ent us done tell you Bess
ent you kinduh 'ooman!

PORGY: [*Frantically*]: Uh don' cyah wuh you t'ink. Weh Bess?

[*They all shrink from telling him. Each evades, trying to leave it
to the others.*]

MARIA: Dat no'count dog, Spo't'n' Life suh you lock'up fuh uh
yeah.

PORGY: Mek somebody ent tell me weh Bess iz?

SERENA: Bess mos' ractify een 'e min' 'kase 'e figguh you lock'up fuh uh yeah. [*Pauses, unable to come to the point.*]

PORGY: Uh home, now! En' Uh wan' tell'um Uh yuh!

SERENA: Bess gone back tuh happy dus' en' likkuh. 'E bin berry drunk fuh two day.

PORGY: Uh ent cyah ef 'e bin drunk! Un wan'um! Weh 'e yiz?

LILY: Dat low down Spo't'n' Life binnuh heng 'roun'um en' mek'um tek mo' happy dus'.

PORGY: [*Driving again to his own door. Calls*]:
Bess! Bess! Nobody wunt tell me!

MARIA: [*Following him*]: Ent us tell you dat houn' Spo't'n' Life-----

PORGY: [*Desperately*]: Uh yent ax 'bout Spo't'n' Life! Weh Bess?

SERENA: 'E gone, Porgy! En' Uh tek dis chile fuh raise' um deestunt!

PORGY: Weh 'e gone?

SERENA: De debble hab'um, fuh true! Dat gal ent nebbuh hab Gawd een 'e haa't.

MARIA: 'E yent de debble! De happy dus' done'um!

PORGY: [*Wildly*]: You mean Bess?---You mean Bess dead?

SERENA: 'E mo' wussuh den dead!

LILY: 'E gone wid Spo't'n' Life 'long de New Yawk boat.
[*They are all silent, gazing at* PORGY. *He, too, is silent for a moment.*]

PORGY: Weh dat iz dey gone?

MINGO: Tuh New Yawk!

MARIA: Dat 'way up een de Nawt'.

PORGY: [*Pointing*]: 'E dat way?

MARIA: 'E tek two day 'long de boat. You cyan' fin'um!

PORGY: Uh yent suh Uh kin fin'um! Uh ax weh 'e yiz!

MARIA: You cyan' gone attuhr'um! Ent us tell you you cyan' fin'um?

ANNIE: Ent you know New Yawk stan' mos' uh t'ous'n mile f'um yuh?

PORGY: W'ich way New Yawk stan'?

LILY: [*Pointing*]: Up nawt' pas' de Custum House!
[PORGY *turns his goat and drives slowly with bowed head toward the gate.*]

MARIA: Porgy, Uh tell you 'e yent no use!

LILY: You cyan' fin'um tuh New Yawk. Dat uh berry big town.

SERENA: Us done tell you, enty?
[*But* PORGY *is going on toward gate as if he did not hear, and they cease to protest and stand motionless watching him.*
As PORGY *reaches the gate,* SCIPIO *silently opens it.* PORGY *drives through and turns to left, as* LILY *pointed.*
St. Michael's chimes the quarter hour. The gate clangs shut.]

CURTAIN

GLOSSARY

This glossary of words and expressions is intended to increase the reader's understanding and appreciation of this particular book. The definitions in this list apply to the dialogue used in this Gullah version of *Porgy*.

One of the characteristic features of the Gullah Language is word usage, that is, some words express different meanings depending on the subject matter.

> e.g.: 1. done fuh---expressing degree as, "Dat gal done fuh oagly."---That girl is extremely ugly.
> 2. done fuh---expressing completed action as, "Uh done fuh cya'um dey dey."---I have already carried it there.

The manner in which Gullah is spoken will vary according to circumstance, and also according to the speaker's idiolect. Sometimes using only one word, a Gullah speaker will express a complete thought.

> e.g.: "Yeddy'um?"---Do, or did you, hear him, her, it, or them?

On another occasion, he/she will leisurely "onrabble 'e mout'."

It's important to remember the two functions of the apostrophe. In this language, the apostrophe does not indicate possession, but rather, the omission of a letter, a word, or several words. The other function of this punctuation mark is to show run-on construction, as: "Wus'den'ebbuh"---worse than ever. The three words are pronounced as one.

The form of a noun does not change to indicate plural number. Verbs are usually expressed in the singular regardless of the number of the noun.

The form of adjectives does not change to show comparison.

The personal pronoun " 'e" expresses him, her, or it. "Um" is them. Medial "r" is usually dropped, as is "g" in present participles. Initial "s" is dropped in the hard consonant combinations "sc," "sp," "sk," "st."

One-syllable prefixes are usually dropped.

Double negatives are constantly used.

The frequent use of idiomatic expressions is a characteristic feature of the Gullah Language, one which makes the language fascinating and at the same time difficult to comprehend. Gullah is one of a group of languages known to dialect geographers as the Atlantic creoles, and is the unique linguistic contribution of the African-American people to our American Heritage.

A

abbuhtize / advertise
agguhnize / agonize
alley cat / à la carte
awgun / organ
ax / ask
ax'um / to ask him, her, it, or them

B

baar / bar
baig / beg
Beefu't / Beaufort, S.C.
bidness / business
bidout / without
bittle / victuals
blin' / blind
bodduh / bother
bo'd'n' house / boarding-house
boxcyaa' / boxcars
buckruh / a white person, or white people
bu'd / bird
bury'n' laa'ge / burying lodge; life insurance company
'buze / abuse
'buze'um / to abuse him, her, it, or them

C

call 'ese'f / pretend
cawcuss / carcass
'cep' / except
chaa'yut / chariot
chupit / stupid
clean gone / having left earlier
clo'es / clothes
co't / court
crack 'e teet' / speak

cum'fuh / come for
cunjuh / conjure
cunwulshun / convulsion
cyaam / calm
cyaaridge / carriage
cyah / care
cyan' / can't
cyan' specify / is not effectual

D

dainjus / dangerous
dayclean / daylight
deestunt / decent
deewo'se / divorce
de't' / death
Dimmycrack / Democrat
done fuh / extremely; or, completed action, as " 'E done fuh gone."
dry long so / for no particular reason

E

'e / he, she, or it
'e stan' so / it is so
eddycashun / education
een / in
ent / is not, are not
en't'ing / and other things (usually of the same category)
enty / is it not so
eye tie up / is fascinated by

F

f'aygrunt / fragrant
farruh / father
Fradjuh / Frazier

freemale / female
fr'en' / friend
fuh true / truly
fus' / first

G

gaud-fayr'n' / God-fearing
gonnil / gunwale
grin' salt / a buzzard circling is grinding salt for his feast
greese 'e mout' / something tasty and fattening to eat
gwi' / going
gwine / going to

H

haa'd / hard
haa'dly'kin / is hardly able
haa'kee / harken; listen to me
haa'm / harm
haa't / heart
hab chile / give birth
happy dus' / dope
hengkilchuh / handkerchief
hice de chune / to begin to sing

I

'il / oil
i'lan' / island

J

jallus / jealous
Josuf / Joseph

K

kyarrysene / kerosene
kibbuhr'um / cover them
kin specify / is effectual
Kittywah / Kiawah

L

lead'um tuh 'e han' / to gain, or have control over
lean fuh / go directly to
leh we go / let's go
lub / love; like
lukkuh / similar

M

man-chile / son
mannussubble / polite
metsidge / message
min'um / take care of him, her, it, or them
mo'nuh / more than
moralize / law-abiding
muskittuh / mosquito
muskle / muscle

N

navuh / neighbor
Nawt' / North
nutt'n' / nothing
nyam / to eat
nyuse'tuh / used to

O

oagly / ugly
obuhreach / outdo

offun / orphan
onnuhrubble / honorable
onrabble 'e mout' / to engage in lengthy conversation; to gossip
'ooman / woman; women
oonuh / you (usually plural)
oshtuh / oyster

P

paa'k / park
pashunt / patience
perrade / parade
pit / put
'plash / splash
plat-eye / an apparition
Prommus Lan' / Promised Land
puhlite / polite
puhwide / provide
'puntop'uh / on top of
pussun / person
pyo' / pure

R

Raatlaige / Rutledge
ractify / ruin
ractify een 'e min' / insane
ramify 'roun' / to behave in a rude or unlawful manner
redduh / rather

S

saa'b / serve
saa'f / soft
Sabannuh / Savannah, Ga.
same lukkuh / the same as

saucuh / saucer
sence / since
sesso / says so
set tuh one side / to sit quietly, and away from other people
shishuh / such a
sho' out / to make a fool of oneself
shum / see him, her, it, or them
silbuh / silver
skrate / straight
soon-man / stylish, or smart man
sosh'ate / associate
sperritual / spiritual
staa'b / starve
stoodun' / student
strain / train
strengk / strength
study 'e head / contemplate
suh / say (also, sir)
sukkumstan' / circumstance
swaytogawd / swear to God
sweet mout' talk / complimentary comments

T

tail tie 'puntop'um / entailed; involved
tangledy / confused
tas'e 'e mout' / tasty food
'tell / until
t'engkgawd / thank God
t'ickit / thicket
't'oruhty / authority
trabble / travel
tuh dat / to that degree, or extent
tuhreckly / directly; soon

W

wabe / wave
waggin / wagon
watuhmilyun / watermelon
w'awf / wharf
waycashun / vacation
we people / family or friends; our people
weh 'e lib / where he lives; his weak point
wissit / visit
wuh / what; that
wu'se / verse
wus'den'ebbuh / worse than ever
w'ymekso / why, or what makes it so

Y

yeddy / hear
yent / same as *ent*, but spelled and pronounced "yent"
when the word follows a soft vowel sound (e.g. Us ent
gwine. 'E yent gwine.) A fast talker will drop the *y* entirely.